Hardening Windows

JONATHAN HASSELL

Hardening Windows
Copyright ©2004 by Jonathan Hassell

ISBN (pbk): 1-59059-266-2

Printed and bound in the United States of America 10987654321

Trademarked names may appear in this book. Rather than use a trademark symbol with every occurrence of a trademarked name, we use the names only in an editorial fashion and to the benefit of the trademark owner, with no intention of infringement of the trademark.

Lead Editor: Jim Sumser

Technical Reviewer: Oris Orlando

Editorial Board: Steve Anglin, Dan Appleman, Gary Cornell, James Cox, Tony Davis, John Franklin, Chris Mills, Steve Rycroft, Dominic Shakeshaft, Julian Skinner, Jim Sumser, Karen Watterson, Gavin Wray, John Zukowski

Project Manager: Tracy Brown Collins

Copy Manager: Nicole LeClerc

Copy Editor: Mark Nigara

Production Manager: Kari Brooks

Production Editor: Janet Vail

Compositor: Dina Quan

Proofreader: Liz Welch

Indexer: Carol Burbo

Artist: April Milne

Cover Designer: Kurt Krames

Manufacturing Manager: Tom Debolski

Distributed to the book trade in the United States by Springer-Verlag New York, Inc., 175 Fifth Avenue, New York, NY 10010 and outside the United States by Springer-Verlag GmbH & Co. KG, Tiergartenstr. 17, 69112 Heidelberg, Germany.

In the United States: phone 1-800-SPRINGER, e-mail orders@springer-ny.com, or visit http://www.springer-ny.com. Outside the United States: fax +49 6221 345229, e-mail orders@springer.de, or visit http://www.springer.de.

For information on translations, please contact Apress directly at 2560 Ninth Street, Suite 219, Berkeley, CA 94710. Phone 510-549-5930, fax 510-549-5939, e-mail info@apress.com, or visit http://www.apress.com.

The information in this book is distributed on an "as is" basis, without warranty. Although every precaution has been taken in the preparation of this work, neither the author(s) nor Apress shall have any liability to any person or entity with respect to any loss or damage caused or alleged to be caused directly or indirectly by the information contained in this work.

The source code for this book is available to readers at http://www.apress.com in the Downloads section.

Contents at a Glance

Contents

About the Author

Jonathan Hassell is a systems administrator and IT consultant residing in Raleigh, NC. He is currently employed by one of the largest departments on campus at North Carolina State University, where he supports a computing environment that consists of Windows NT, 2000, XP, Server 2003, Sun Solaris, and HP-UX machines.

Hassell has extensive experience in networking technologies and Internet connectivity. He currently runs his own web-hosting business, Enable Hosting, which is based out of both Raleigh and Charlotte, NC. He is involved in all facets of the business, including finances, marketing, operating decisions, and customer relations.

Jonathan's previous published work includes *RADIUS*, published by O'Reilly & Associates, which serves as a detailed guide to the RADIUS authentication protocol and offers suggestions for implementing RADIUS and overall network security. He has also written monthly columns for the *Windows 2000 Magazine Network* and WindowsITSecurity.com. His work has also been published in CMP's *Publish* magazine and Pinnacle's *Linux AppDev* newsletter. Hassell's latest book, *Managing Windows Server 2003*, will be published by O'Reilly & Associates in early 2004.

About the Technical Reviewer

Oris Orlando, born in Naples, Italy, in 1971, has been interested in computer science since the eighties. His first computer was an Intellivision Computer Module, which allowed him to develop programs in the limited edition BASIC language only. At the end of the eighties, he began to use 8086 machines, and in 1989 he enrolled in the computer science department at the University of Salerno (Italy), from which he graduated in 1997. During his university career, he developed many applications for small businesses and often used a bulletin board system (BBS), before the Internet grew in popularity. In December 1997 he worked at Siemens Nixdorf for two years as an analyst and programmer (Java, C, PL/SQL, CGI, HTML) in a web environment. In 1999 he took a position at Bull HN, where, for the first two years he belonged to a technical team. By the third year he became the project leader in the security department, before eventually becoming project manager. He is experienced in UNIX, Windows, Linux, DOS, computer programming, the Internet, security, and databases (Oracle, LDAP).

Acknowledgments

THIS BOOK WAS WRITTEN BY ME, but that is arguably the smallest part of the job. This tome was made possible and put together by a score of people other than me, and they all deserve praise and gratitude. First, my sincere appreciation goes to my editor, Jim Sumser, for his role in this work. Jim is a fabulous, flexible, and understanding guy, and I'm thankful for my opportunities to work with him. Also thanks to Tracy Brown Collins and Mark Nigara, both at Apress, who corrected my mistakes, kept me on schedule, and worked with me during a very busy period.

Also thanks to Oris Orlando for his timely and helpful comments upon reviewing the manuscript. Although he worked to point out mistakes and deficiencies in coverage, any errors and omissions that remain are mine and mine alone.

And finally, but certainly not least important, my significant other Lisa had the patience of a saint during this process and made the entire experience a lot easier on me. Thanks for all that you do for me. This one is for you.

Introduction

BEFORE I BEGIN, LET ME OFFER my sincere thanks for purchasing this book! I'm glad you've made the decision to spend some time securing and hardening your systems. Not only are you helping yourself, but you're protecting the Internet community as a whole.

Hardening Windows is organized into chapters that focus on different aspects of system hardening. Chapters 2, 3, and 4 describe procedures related to specific versions of Windows. This isn't to say that the techniques described in one chapter for one version of Windows can't be used on another: It's simply a matter of organizing the flow of the book so you get the most from each chapter. The remaining chapters focus on different issues that affect the security and integrity of your systems and networks. At the end of each chapter, you'll find a list of checkpoints, which summarize in a sentence or two each strategy discussed within the chapter. I've collected a list of checkpoints from every chapter and put them in Appendix A for easy reference.

This book is quick and simple, so it's best to understand what's inside before you even begin reading it. For one, the chapters themselves stand alone. You can read them in any order, and the material isn't cumulative. Of course, you're welcome to read them all, and cross-references are clearly identified when information in a chapter is discussed in more detail earlier in the book. However, if you choose to begin with Chapter 7, you won't be missing anything. You also won't be getting long, theoretical discussions about operating-system design, kernel locking, OSI layers, and the like. Instead, you're getting quick, practical, checklist-style suggestions with a minimum of fluff. This book is meant to be carried under your arm to client workstations, placed on the top of the server rack, or snugly kept right beside your monitor for easy reference. It certainly isn't a 1600-page Windows bible.

Let me briefly address another issue: There are, of course, any number of hardening methods, and any number of opinions on how effective those methods are. This book would never be complete if it attempted to describe every view of every way to possibly secure a system from an unknown threat. Instead, I've chosen to keep the book short, using proven, time-tested ways to achieve maximum protection for the time and money invested. I think you'll find the results more than acceptable.

In short, you have 145 suggestions for hardening your system—which averages one checkpoint per page in this book. I hope this book helps you harden your systems, and I hope you consider it a worthwhile investment. Thanks for reading.

CHAPTER 1

Hardening: Theory and General Practice

You should be exactly as paranoid as it is cost-effective to be.

—Scott Collins

THESE ARE WISE WORDS from security expert Scott Collins, and they serve as the underlying motivation behind this book.

Computer security seems to be making the news a lot lately. Almost every week, malevolent forces crawl out of the woodwork to take down high-profile websites. Companies lose millions of dollars and suffer damage to computer systems. As a result, large companies spend thousands of dollars on security systems and products to protect the doors to their corporate networks. Microsoft recently bore the brunt of two intruder attacks on its web properties. The result was hours of downtime and decreased customer confidence.

It's hard to know the number of intruders currently threatening the computer realm. Many systems administrators and users have built up a tolerance to attempted hacking. They have accepted intruders as the norm, as by-products of using a directly connected system. Many attempts, whether successful or not, go unnoticed by users. Internet security experts agree, though, that the number of attempts at security breaches is increasing, as is the sophistication and efficiency of the attempts. To keep up, vendors and security hardware manufacturers struggle to plug the security holes that intruders uncover and exploit with today's easy-to-use system-cracking tools.

An intruder attack is only one facet of security with which you should be concerned. Viruses are another big security threat; the fact that they spread easily only increases their infestations. For example, worm viruses spread when users open email attachments, which cause the virus to email itself to the user's entire contact list. Other Trojan horse viruses can come into your system and leave a back door for intruders who will use your computer to make countless attacks on other users' machines.

Helping you learn how to protect your computing environment from these various threats is the purpose of this book. System administrators all around the world know the Internet is a hostile environment. They can't tell when a hacker will attempt to gain access to the SQL server, but they can bet that there will be an attempt soon. Because the operating system is vital to a computer's functioning, and because it's the only layer between the machine's available resources and its users, it's critical that the OS resists compromise.

Hardening is this process of protecting a system against unknown threats. System administrators harden against whatever they think could be a threat. This book is designed to provide a quick and easy checklist-style reference for system administrators who need to anticipate those attacks and compromises. You'll need to harden Windows NT, 2000, XP, and Server 2003 against these threats. And in this chapter, I'll look at the theories behind security and hardening a system, and how you can take very general approaches to overall organizational security before investigating specific hardening practices on your Windows client and server machines.

What Is Security?

To protect the well-being or integrity of something, to ensure the safety of property or interests in an object from intrusion, or to keep a concept or object private, you'll need to secure a system. In the hostile environment of the Internet, system administrators need to restrict access to assets. To grant access to a selected group of users, you need to know who to trust and how to verify the credentials of—authenticate—those you allow to use your systems.

The cornerstones of any security policy include the following:

- Privacy, or the ability to keep things private and confidential

- Trust, or the question of whether you should take data or objects at face value

- Authenticity, or verifying that contacts are made with people who are accurately representing their identity

- Integrity, or the process of ensuring a system hasn't yet been compromised and will remain secure

This book will focus entirely on the practical aspects of hardening a Windows-based computer. What are these practical checkpoints, which comprise the rest of this book, designed to do? What is the underlying motivation? Focusing for a bit on the more general aspects of computer security allows you to harden your systems in ways that you might otherwise ignore or fail to imagine. Therefore, I'll discuss security and its associated theoretical issues, and then move into practical considerations that aren't limited to just Windows machines—suggestions that are appropriate for any connected machine.

The Security Dilemma

Security depends on two things: First, a person must define what security means for them, and second, that person must communicate that idea clearly and competently to the community around him. Security suffers from such a problem these days because of issues related directly to these two requirements. Security for each person is different. Though one person may be satisfied with a BIOS password and a floppy disk, another person might take great pains to double- and triple-encrypt files. She may wish to transfer them only over IPsec-protected links, and purchase trusted Secure Sockets Layer (SSL) certificates for any type of public service she offers. And because the definition, meaning, and intrinsic value of security differs so wildly between parties, it's difficult to communicate a clear security policy to the user community. Therein lies a critical problem—you can only have effective security when everyone understands the level of security required and when everyone agrees security is necessary. And in practice, as you might imagine, an understanding of security on the part of the user is something that's usually severely lacking.

The very existence of security resides in trust. In fact, it can be argued that every security problem boils down to the simplest level as a question of trust. The idea of security is introduced for the sole purpose of protecting yourself against parties whom you don't trust. To do this, usually some kind of technology is put into place to move trust from a risky "zone" to a safer, more palatable area. A great example is a front door lock: You don't trust the general public, and therefore you're wary of them stealing your belongings without your knowledge. You install a lock on the front door of your house. You still don't trust the general public, but you trust the lock to do its job to keep the untrusted people out. You obviously have less of a problem trusting the lock than trusting the intentions of a great number of people to whom you're unaccustomed. You can't fully trust the lock either, so you install an alarm system that notifies the police if someone breaks in. You've displaced your trust from the public to the police, the alarm system, and the lock.

Each day, you proceed about your business, placing your trust semiconsciously in banks, automated teller machines, online shopping sites, the police, all levels of government, and other various establishments. The list goes on and on. You don't question this trust, because it's seldom broken, but that isn't always the end result. For example, when a child learns to drive a car, he places lives at risk. Because of this risk, most municipalities and governments require the child to pass an exam to demonstrate her mastery of the safe operation of the equipment. Computer systems are equally capable of causing great damage, even though they aren't sentient. Your life is interrupted when computer systems malfunction, and this indicates an increasing reliance on them. Your trust in computers and their users is often quite misplaced. This is where the problems truly come from.

Enemies of Security

To achieve truer security, system administrators need to examine a method for analyzing systems to probe their weaknesses and detail their own assumptions about those systems' security, rather than blindly placing trust in them. If security is to be discussed in a more serious way, there needs to be the following:

- Identification of what one is trying to protect

- Evaluation of the main sources of risk and where trust is placed

- Assumption of possible countermeasures to potential attacks

You can define a secure system as one in which all of the threats have been analyzed and one in which countermeasures are in place for all of the threats. There are a few stumbling blocks that hinder your ability to create secure systems. The first is complexity: Users will become impatient and work around security if it becomes too cumbersome for their work style and flow. Next is the need for backward compatibility in software. Often security is tightened in later revisions of software, but to remain operable with the previous version of a package, security restrictions might be loosened. Additionally, backups create a somewhat obscure but very real hole. The fact that backups are usually conducted with redundancy in mind might translate to more opportunity for data to be stolen. Security must be applied to backups as well as normal operations.

The problem, however, is how to know what all of the possible threats against a system are. That's where this book comes in. You can't always know all of your threats; it's impossible to have that sort of knowledge. But you can batten down the hatches and take precautions to forestall and thwart any future attempted intrusions.

Some General Hardening Suggestions

In the rest of this chapter, I'll discuss some points that you can consider to harden your network overall. I've broken them down into three encompassing categories: software, hardware, and network considerations. Again, the following aren't meant to be specific suggestions; they're meant more as broad launching points for the specific checkpoints presented later in this book, and for future improvements to the integrity of your network that you can make on your own.

Software Considerations

Let's begin with the behemoth: service packs. Service packs are applications that are released after the public release of a software package. More specifically, they're collections of hotfixes, or patches to flaws that are found after an application's mainstream availability. Most of these service packs include security to correct areas of the program code that weren't secured by the developers and therefore have vulnerabilities. You can be sure that your system will be examined by nefarious users looking for these vulnerabilities; you can be equally certain new vulnerabilities are being searched out as you read this by these same miscreants. The bottom line: Keep all machines on the network updated and check with the operating system and application vendors on a regular basis for service releases and hotfix patches.

Next on the list are viruses, a rapidly growing irritation. As you may be aware, many new viruses are released weekly. Because of this, if an Internet connection comes anywhere near any machine, you should use antivirus software. It should be kept up-to-date on a regular basis. To protect yourself, take a look at these guidelines:

- Any software downloaded from the Internet should be stored and installed on test systems before any production deployment, and the system should be scanned for viruses after the software has been tested.

- Like safe sex, don't download software from unknown sources; a prominent violation of this policy is the retrieval of programs from peer-to-peer file transfer services. This not only endangers the host computer, but the entire network. Lately, viruses are beginning spread after initial execution onto network shares and, depending on the strain of virus, it can cause many hours of downtime, which results in a significant financial liability.

- For best results, you should configure your virus software to the most restrictive level, thereby ensuring that any virus activity is contained to one computer without infecting the network.

- Most modern antivirus programs include the option to attempt to repair an infected file—you will likely have mixed results with this feature. It's acceptable to repair the infected file for a period of time so that the system can become operational.

- As a matter of practice, I always recommend that infected systems be wiped clean and reinstalled from an empty hard disk as soon as possible. As hard as the antivirus companies try, they may never completely penetrate a virus's payload; they might not ever realize the true extent of a virus's damage to a system, so to be safe, restarting the system from a known clean baseline is always the cheapest insurance.

- Block all potentially malicious file types, such as VBS, EXE, COM, and SCR, from your mail server. These file types are rarely used for legitimate business purposes and can accidentally be executed by unsuspecting users. This can compromise your entire network. Remember the Melissa virus?

- Set your antivirus to scan the selected extension for virus patterns that may exist. This ensures that a virus doesn't slip past your firewall.

Hardware and Network Considerations

In this section, you'll look at some considerations about hardening your hardware. Because this book focuses on Windows, it doesn't contain room anywhere else for these kinds of suggestions, but I'd be remiss not to include them. In any case, Windows depends as much on external hardware devices for security as it does on its own internal mechanisms.

The most obvious piece of the physical-device puzzle is the firewall, an integral part of any network that is connected to the Internet. Without a firewall, any Internet-connected machine can be subjected to denial-of-service attacks, targeted service attacks, network-penetration efforts, and other bad events. All of these attacks are very difficult to trace back to their origin, too, making a "forensic analysis" next to impossible. Consider the following firewall suggestions:

- Block TCP ports 135, 139, and 445, and UDP ports 135, 137, and 445. These are Microsoft Windows's networking ports that have been traditionally vulnerable to a great many distributed service attacks, and there's little use for them over the Internet.

- Block all other unused ports. Each time you open a port you create a hole in the wall that you've built around your network, and you replace it with a window. The more ports you open—the more windows you install in your wall—the more transparent your network becomes to the outside. The bottom line? Open ports invite attacks.

The firewall's brother in the security family is an intrusion detection system (IDS), another vital part of hardening a Windows-based network. An IDS "sniffs out" or inspects all traffic going in and coming out of a network, and distinguishes patterns inside that traffic that could indicate suspicious activity. An IDS differs from a firewall in that a firewall looks for intrusions in order to stop them from happening. The firewall limits the access between networks in order to prevent intrusion and doesn't signal an attack from inside the network. An IDS, on the other hand, evaluates a suspected intrusion once it has taken place, and signals an alarm. An IDS also watches for attacks that originate from within a system. It's a beneficial addition to your network, and I highly recommend it.

Remote access remains one of the weakest links in network security if it's incorrectly implemented, and in many cases it's the holy grail for intruders looking to do damage. If you allow remote access to your network either through dial-up connections or through a virtual private network (VPN) connection, you should restrict dial-up access to trusted users, and limit the functionality of those users from remote locations. Policies can be designed in such a way that user activity will be traced. I would recommend a VPN connection: Data that travels over a VPN is much less susceptible to interception than normal point-to-point protocol (PPP) connections over the plain old telephone networks. If your data is particularly critical, you might consider putting systems in place that require credential validation for any resource that is accessed remotely, like client-side certificates and strong password authentication methods.

Also, it's a safe bet to say that intruders would rather use the convenience and availability of the Internet than work harder at "war dialing," which is when an intruder generates phone numbers on a random basis and dials them to see if a modem answers. However, if your business needs require a modem bank to answer incoming calls, you might consider mandating a dial-back setting to a predetermined number; this is a great way to ensure that a connection is made only between the appropriate parties.

Physical segmentation of the network is always a good choice for security. If your hardware devices allow you to perform this segregation easily, then there's little reason to not segment them. Virtual LANs (VLANs) are a great way to wall off large sections of your network. If you place your firewall within a separate VLAN from your network and specify that only your firewall can access your network, then you've just eliminated the chance that an intruder could use another window of entry into your network. Segmenting a network can also add an element of security from an internal perspective, because you can segment a network in such a way that all users can see the servers but no user can see each other. This reduces the possibility of hacking user data stored on user machines and greatly reduces the chance of a virus spreading around the computers. If the virus code can't find other computers to infect, it cannot spread.

I feel compelled to include this bit here, even though a later chapter is devoted completely to Internet Information Services (IIS) hardening tips, because it's so vital to security. Many exploits are targeted against IIS because it's a very generic and widely used web server, and it's left on by default in most instances. Because of this prevalence of worms, which travel at great speeds and exploit unsecured IIS web servers on publicly accessible networks, it's highly recommended—imperative, even. Systems running IIS should be installed on an isolated network segment, or with no network cable attached, until the latest service packs and hotfixes are installed. Microsoft has published an IIS Lockdown tool, which is now part of the Microsoft Baseline Security Analyzer for Windows 2000 Server computers running IIS. It's very important that this tool be used to harden the IIS box.

Checkpoints

In this chapter, I've discussed theories about security, and I've also listed some very broad, general suggestions for hardening the hardware, network, and software owned by your organization. Here's a recap of what's been covered so far:

- Learn the cornerstones of good security policy: privacy, trust, authentication, and integrity.

- Understand the social implications of security.

- Recognize the security dilemma—that users must understand the need for security and agree to the extent to which security is implemented.

- Consider transfers of trust in security policy.

- Understand the process of defining the concept of security: identification of the object to protect, evaluation of risk, and proposals for countermeasures to potential attacks.

- Recognize some of the enemies of a secure system: complexity, backward compatibility, backups.

- Embrace the role that hardening takes in protecting against unknown threats.

- Apply service packs to operating systems and applications throughout your company.

- Purchase, install, and keep updated antivirus software installed throughout your company networks.

- Test and scan new downloads, and practice safe computing when transferring files from public networks.

- Wipe virus-infected systems to a clean hard disk as soon as possible.

- Block malicious file attachments as they enter your network at the email server, before it reaches the client.

- Install a firewall and close off networking ports (TCP 135, 139, and 445; UDP 135, 137, and 445) and any other unused ports.

- Consider the purchase and installation of an intrusion detection system.

- Properly restrict access to remote entry points to your network, and encourage the use of virtual private networks over traditional telephonic and modem connections.

- Implement dial-back for standard telephone connections.

- Investigate the physical segmentation of your network.

- Properly harden and secure any IIS systems on the network, and relegate IIS systems to a blocked-off segment of the network during the installation of patches.

- Read the rest of this book.

CHAPTER 2

Windows NT Security

WINDOWS NT, BY VIRTUE of its age, is vulnerable to all sorts of attacks, from both outside and in. The most effective way to harden your NT system is to attack the problem of insecurity from several different perspectives, especially passwords, account policies, virus protection, and system policies. This chapter will give you the tools you need to achieve a reasonably hardened NT system in exchange for a bit of effort.

Windows NT System Policy Editor

Akin to Group Policy, which is found in Windows 2000 and later versions, System Policies in Windows NT provide a more effective way of applying and enforcing a common set of settings and security definitions across a domain of computers. It's certainly not as customizable, flexible, easy-to-use, or scalable as Group Policy, but it's still quite a bit better than manually applying hundreds of changes to multiple computers.

TIP *You can apply most of the methods and hardening strategies covered in later sections of this chapter to multiple computers using NT system policies.*

Windows NT loads with a default system policy in effect that continues to dictate which settings are in force whether it's modified or not. You can view this policy and make the changes by using the NT System Policy Editor, which you can access by selecting Start ➢ Run ➢ PolEdit. Once you've launched the program, two icons are displayed: Default User and Default Computer. These apply to all computers and all users in a domain, whereas more specific policies can apply to certain users, groups, and computers (for instance, specific departments of users or specific machines in a given location).

When you double-click any given policy object, boxes are raised on the screen. Here, you can make changes to individual aspects of the policy. There are three states to each individual policy setting, and you can cycle through each one by repeatedly clicking the box until the desired state appears. The three states are defined as follows:

- Settings turned on appear with a checked box beside the text describing the function of the settings.

- Settings turned off appear with an unchecked box beside the text.

- Settings that have never been defined, and therefore are unused, appear with a grayed-out box.

There's an important distinction to be made between settings that are disabled and settings that have no previous state set. Unused settings have no effect on system behavior, whereas unchecked settings, which signify that the particular policies are disabled, do affect the operation of NT in one way or another. Unused settings instruct NT to default to a particular Registry value that will define the settings' operation for that session. At the same time the unused settings will simultaneously set or disable options in the policy override Registry settings. For example, if the Run Logon Scripts Simultaneously policy is grayed out, the default settings in the Registry will take over. If the box is checked, then multiple scripts will absolutely run at the same time. However, if the box is unchecked, then multiple scripts will never run at the same time.

Customizing and Applying Group Policies

You can transfer settings between users, groups, and computers by cutting and pasting policies. This process makes a replica of the settings for the individual units. You can also apply system policies to multiple computers by taking advantage of the System Policies Update setting under the Network category. There are two modes by which multiple computers can gain access to and subsequently apply a set of system policies:

- Automatic mode, in which the remote computers contact a computer specified as the policy server, which is a primary domain controller, and download a file called NTCONFIG.POL from the NETLOGON share of that domain controller. This is automatic in that most domain controllers are always available. You can also ensure more availability by checking the Load Balancing box, which instructs clients to contact the backup domain controllers for a copy of the file in the event the PDC is unavailable. You can configure the NT File Replication Service to migrate the NTCONFIG.POL file to backup domain controllers (BDCs) on the network automatically.

- Manual mode, in which the remote computers download a policy file (which can be named anything—there are no restrictions) from any computer on the network. This is more haphazard, because domain controllers are known to be the most available computers on the network, so users might encounter error messages if policy files are hosted on machines that are turned off frequently or otherwise disconnected from the network.

With regard to permissions, users need to be able to read these files. Administrators should be able to read and write them, and they should also own them.

Resolving Conflicts Between Multiple Policies

Conflicts between policies—for example, the Default User policy, which allows changes to a desktop background against a specific department policy prohibiting the same—are resolved according to an administrator's specification. You can make this specification by selecting Group Priority on the Options menu. The orders of groups are determined here, and you can select which groups have priority over others by moving the selected groups up and down in the list using the appropriate buttons on the right side of the window.

NOTE   *It's important to remember that user-specific policies always trump any group-specific policies, regardless of the order in which they are specified in the Group Priority box.*

TIP   *To make your life easier, you should apply policies only to groups. If there's a need to apply a policy to a specific person, consider creating a group and put that person in it. This strategy makes policies much more manageable.*

Recommended User Policy Settings

There are several critical policy settings that you should immediately define, as shown in Tables 2.1 and 2.2.

Table 2.1 Critical User Policy Settings

SETTING	LOCATION	DISABLED FEATURE	RECOMMENDED SETTING
Deny access to display icon	Control Panel/Display/Restrict Display	Disables user access to the Control Panel display icon	Disabled
Hide Screen Saver tab	Control Panel/Display/Restrict Display	Disables user access to the Screen Saver tab inside the Display applet	Enabled
Wallpaper	Desktop	Restricts what wallpaper a user can choose to set as his desktop background	Disabled
Remove Run command from Start menu	Shell/Restrictions	Removes command-line access for user	Enabled
Remove folders from Settings on Start menu	Shell/Restrictions	Removes access to Control Panel and Printers control panel applets directly from Start menu	Enabled
Remove taskbar from Settings on Start menu	Shell/Restrictions	Removes access to customizations for the taskbar and Start menu	Enabled
Remove Find command from Start menu	Shell/Restrictions	Takes away Find command from Start menu, thereby hindering user ability to search for files on hard disk and network	Enabled
Hide drives in My Computer	Shell/Restrictions	Restricts display of local drives from within My Computer	Enabled
Hide Network Neighborhood	Shell/Restrictions	Restricts display of NetBIOS-based browse requests within the Windows user interface	Enabled

Table 2.1 Critical User Policy Settings (Continued)

SETTING	LOCATION	DISABLED FEATURE	RECOMMENDED SETTING
No Entire Network in Network Neighborhood	Shell/Restrictions	Disables browsing beyond the local subnet inside Network Neighborhood	Enabled
Hide all items on desktop	Shell/Restrictions	Restricts display of any icons on the desktop; most appropriate for a kiosk environment	Enabled
Disable Shut Down command	Shell/Restrictions	Prevents rebooting or powering off the machine	Disabled
Don't save settings at Exit	Shell/Restrictions	Disables the default function of Windows Explorer to save changes made to the local user environment	Enabled
Disable Registry editing tools	System/Restrictions	Prevents the local copy of the program RedEdt32 from being run on the local machine; it doesn't prevent its execution from CD-ROM or from a network share	Enabled
Run only allowed Windows applications	System/Restrictions	Specifies a list of names of acceptable programs a user may launch; the matching is rudimentary and can be thwarted by renaming any executable to an acceptable name	Enabled with a specific, limited list of applications
Only use approved shell extensions	Windows NT Shell/ Restrictions	Disables the use of TweakUI (a Windows Power Toy) and other shell add-ons	Enabled
Disable context menus for the taskbar	Windows NT Shell/ Restrictions	Disables right-clicking the taskbar to take advantage of shell functionality	Enabled

Table 2.1 Critical User Policy Settings (Continued)

SETTING	LOCATION	DISABLED FEATURE	RECOMMENDED SETTING
Remove common programs groups from Start menu	Windows NT Shell/ Restrictions	Takes away the program groups with (Common) appended to them in the Start menu, such as Administrative Tools and Games	Enabled
Remove Map Network Drive and Disconnect Network Drive options	Windows NT Shell/ Restrictions	Disables mapping drives to specific network locations	Enabled
Parse AUTOEXEC.BAT	Windows NT System	Determines if AUTOEXEC.BAT is used to enable search paths for the current session	Enabled
Run logon scripts synchronously	Windows NT System	Determines if multiple logon scripts, provided they exist, will be executed at the same time	Enabled
Disable Task Manager	Windows NT System	Enables or disables access to the Task Manager	Enabled
Show welcome tips at logon	Windows NT System	Determines whether or not system and user tips are displayed upon a user logging on to the system	Disabled

Table 2.2. Critical Computer Policy Settings

SETTING	LOCATION	DISABLED FEATURE	RECOMMENDED SETTING
Run	System/Run	Lists programs to be run at logon	List only necessary programs
Create hidden drive shares	Windows NT Network/Sharing	Prohibits using "$" at the end of a share name to hide a share from view through casual browsing	Enabled
Scheduler priority	Windows NT Printers	Defines the priority of the print service against all other running processes during a session	Set a reasonable priority according to the other purposes of the machine in question
Logon banner	Windows NT System/Logon	Defines and displays a message presented to users when they press Ctrl-Alt-Del to log on to an NT system	Set to your unauthorized-use or acceptable-use policy
Enable shutdown from Authentication dialog box	Windows NT System/Logon	Enables or disables the Shut Down button on the username and password screen	Enabled
Do not display last logged on username	Windows NT System/Logon	Defines whether the username field is populated with the username of the last successful logon	Enabled
Run logon scripts synchronously	Windows NT System/Logon	Gives complete user-level access to logon scripts so that they don't fail out with insufficient permissions	Enabled

Passwords

It's arguable but completely believable that passwords are the weakest link in any security system. With more powerful computers working at faster speeds, what used to be a nearly impossible task—password cracking—has now become not quite trivial, but indeed much simpler. So it's always important that your users choose good passwords that will cause difficulty to automated cracker programs.

> **NOTE**   *For examples of good passwords, check out the passprop utility, which is included in the Windows NT Resource Kit. This small program will generate high-quality, random passwords that you can use within your organization or distribute as a model to your users.*

Password Policies

Of course, you can't teach old dogs new tricks, which is why you sometimes need to force your users into compliance. Here are several suggestions for a stringent policy that won't cause an uprising among your users:

- **Maximum password age:** 90 days. This forces your users to change to a unique password every given interval. If you set this for too long of an interval, an attacker has an increased chance of obtaining a current password, but if you set it for too short of an interval, you'll waste your security budget answering complaints about why your users have to change their passwords again. It also increases the chance of passwords on sticky notes attached to monitors, and you all know that isn't a good thing.

- **Minimum password age:** 1 day. More clever users may discover that, without this setting, they can circumvent the password-age requirement by changing their password as mandated by the policy, and then immediately change the password back to their preferred phrase. Using this option requires the user to keep the changed password for at least one day before changing it back.

- **Minimum password length:** Eight characters. It's easy to compute the probability that a three-letter password could be guessed in fewer permutations (and thus more rapidly) than a longer password. This is a surprisingly effective front against persistent password-cracking attempts.

- **Password uniqueness:** Five passwords. Windows will store a list of a user's previous passwords in the Registry. Setting this option prevents the person from alternating between two common passwords, thereby forcing them to be creative and not reuse old passwords that may have been cracked.

- **Account lockout:** Locks after five failed attempts; resets counter after 10 minutes. There exists software for hackers that will attempt "brute force" attacks on user accounts, using a list of common passwords and a dictionary to attempt to crack an account over and over again. The lockout feature disables an account after a given number of attempts with failed passwords. The feature also includes a counter that resets the number of attempts.

- **Lockout duration:** 15 minutes. This option goes hand in hand with the previous configuration. The lockout duration feature resets accounts disabled by the account lockout feature. It's important to remember the fundamental economic concept that idle users equal lost money. In a small business, this isn't as much of an issue, because the administrator is usually available for five minutes to unlock a disabled account, but in organizations with thousands of sloppy typists, it can make for a large help-desk budget. Use with caution.

Password Cracking

Although it may seem like venturing to the dark side, a sage administrator can use the enemy's tools against the enemy himself. There are numerous password-cracker utilities available for download on the Internet. The resounding favorite among most "white-hat" cracker administrators is PwDump, which can run through an NT system's SAM database, pick out the passwords, and list them in a text dump in a format much like the /etc/passwd file you would find on a UNIX-esque system.

However, this next bit goes to show that passwords simply cannot be your only line of defense. The folks that run the site http://lasecpc13.epfl.ch/ntcrack/ have developed a Windows NT/2000/XP password cracker that can crack any alphanumeric password in five seconds (or ten seconds if the password is longer than seven characters). What's amazing is that this cracker doesn't require a Linux-based Beowulf cluster or a supercomputer. It runs on an AMD Athlon XP 2500+ system with 1.5 GB of RAM. The really scary part is that they've posted a web page that allows you to enter an NT/2000/XP password hash, which you can obtain using the PwDump utility, and after a five-second wait get the corresponding password.

There is a fix, though, if temporary. Change your NT/2000/XP passwords that contain only numbers and letters so that they also include at least one other nonalphanumeric character. Their cracker won't crack such passwords. Obviously, that's an artificial limitation. They could just as easily have calculated their large lookup tables with those nonalphanumeric password characters included.

Protecting User Accounts

Though passwords are important gate sentries, they aren't the only method of safeguarding a system. Windows NT provides an operating system security feature called Account Policies, which let you set restrictions on various properties of a user account.

- Rename the administrator account carefully. The administrator account is of course a popular target for crackers. By renaming the administrator account to something less obvious, you can reduce a very probable attack vector. However, this isn't a surefire solution. You must be careful of any server products on your machine that require use of the administrator account—by renaming the account, you can break the server products beyond repair, thereby necessitating a reformat or reinstall on your server.

- Remove the Everyone group from the access control lists (ACLs) and add the Authenticated Users group in its place. This is an easy fix that won't ruin any functionality on your machine. By default, Windows NT is installed with ACLs that allow reading and writing by anyone on the computer, whether that user is authenticated or not. Obviously this is a problem, because attackers on a larger network can connect to the box via standard Windows file sharing, map to a default administrative share like C$, and then have their way with any files on the drive. When you replace Everyone with Authenticated Users, only those who identify themselves to the computer with credentials that pass the checks of the local system authority are allowed access.

- Disable the Guest account. Few legitimate applications require access to the Guest account, and it's a big hole in the security of a machine. The main problem with the Guest account is that you have no sense of who used the account and what that user did with it—there is no auditing or accountability for the actions performed with that account, which makes it infinitely more difficult to track down possible infiltrations and nefarious activity.

Registry Procedures

The Registry is a boon to system administrators and a gold mine to undesirables. Most every aspect of the operation of a Windows NT system is controlled by the keys, values, and hives contained therein. The following six Registry modifications are the most effective ways to significantly harden the "under the hood" functionality of NT.

- Disable remote access and control of the Registry, or at the very minimum tightly control it. (HKLM\CurrentControlSet\Control\SecurePipeServers\ Winreg, value 1; HKLM\System\CurrentControlSet\Services\ LanManServer\Parameters\NullSessionPipes, value <Configure with authorized names>)

- Disable the display of the username of the last person to have used the system. (HKLM\SOFTWARE\Microsoft\Windows NT\Current Version\WinLogin\DontDisplayLastUserName, value 1)

- Set tight permissions on the security event log. (HKLM\System\ CurrentControlSet\Services\EventLog\[LogName]\RestrictGuestAccess, value 1)

- Set tight permissions on printers and printer drivers, particularly those associated with certain sensitive roles, such as invoicing and check production. (HKLM\System\CurrentControlSet\Control\Print\ Providers\LanManPrintServices\Servers, value 1)

- Disable anonymous logins, particularly their ability to list account names. (HKLM\System\CurrentControlSet\Control\LSAName\RestrictAnonymous, value 1)

- Set tight permissions on the ability to set scheduled tasks, either via the Windows GUI or through the command-line AT tool. (HKLM\System\ CurrentControlSet\Control\Lsa\SubmitControl, value 1; HKLM\System\ CurrentControlSet\Services\Schedule, value <Restrict access to administrators>)

Protecting the File System

Once an attacker is in a system, she can still be thwarted by establishing proper, secure file-system permissions, which are critical to fully hardening any system on any network.

Locking Down Local Directories

Table 2-3 contains a list of the most common files and directories on a Windows NT system and the suggested permissions that the group Everyone (or the group Authenticated Users, if you've taken the advice in this chapter) should have. These tend to be very restrictive, thereby reducing the surface through which a data attack could take place.

Table 2-3. Suggested Permissions for the Everyone (or Authenticated Users) Group

PATH	SUGGESTED PERMISSIONS FOR EVERYONE
C:\	List
C:*.*	No access if possible, read if absolutely necessary
C:\WINNT	Read
C:\WINNT\SYSTEM32	Read
C:\WINNT\SYSTEM32\CONFIG	List or no access at all
C:\WINNT\SYSTEM32\SPOOL\PRINTERS	Read or list (change for owners)
C:\WINNT\SYSTEM32*.DLL	Read
C:\WINNT\SYSTEM32*.EXE	Read
C:\WINNT\SYSTEM	Read
C:\WINNT\SYSTEM*.DRV	Read
C:\WINNT\SYSTEM*.DLL	Read
C:\WINNT\PIF	Read
C:\WINNT\REPAIR	No access at all
C:\WINNT\PROFILES	Add, read
C:\WINNT*.EXE	Read
C:\WINNT\PROFILES\ALL USERS	Read
C:\WINNT\PROFILES\DEFAULT USER	Read
C:\WINNT\PROFILES\ADMINISTRATOR	No access
Within C:\WINNT\PROFILES	No access at all (except full control for owners)
C:\TEMP	Read, write, change, execute

Table 2-3. Suggested Permissions for the Everyone (or Authenticated Users) Group (Continued)

PATH	SUGGESTED PERMISSIONS FOR EVERYONE
Program File Directories	List or read
Home Folders for Users	List or no access at all (read, write, execute, own for owners)

Search Paths

Ever since the days of UNIX and DOS there has been an operating-system feature called the path, which is simply a list of directories on the file system that the OS should search when an executable file is called from the command line without reference to its full path. Though this is definitely convenient, it's also possible for a user to replace an NT system file with a nefarious program and thereby have it called from the command line accidentally.

There are a couple of ways to prevent this:

- Ensure that system directories come before anything else in the search path. This way, when NT looks for an executable called from the command line, it will find the version in the system directory first.

- Lock the system directory down. Remove write access from groups that don't need it, particularly on system and program-file directories. Also, lock user directories down in the same manner.

Guarding Against Internet Threats

Windows NT comes out of the box unreasonably insecure. Despite the fact that NT itself has significant programming flaws that make the operating system code itself insecurely (a fact that Microsoft officially acknowledged when it terminated support for the Workstation edition in mid-2003), it also installs with defaults that basically indicate to a would-be Internet attacker, "I am wide open. Have your way with me."

This section covers two significant methods you can use to harden an NT system: filtering TCP/IP ports to reduce the risk of a port-vectored attack, and establishing a virus protection regimen to reduce the risk of Trojan horse, worm, and virus infiltration.

Windows NT Port Filtering

Windows NT comes with a rudimentary port filter that allows you to discard incoming packets based on their destination protocol and the protocol by which they were sent. You can access this port-filtering utility through the TCP/IP Properties page inside the Network control panel. Inside the Properties page, click the Advanced button of the pertinent IP address and then check the Enable Security box and click Configure.

Though the port filtering provided within NT certainly isn't an enterprise-class firewall, it's helpful when you have a machine that has sensitive data on it and ought to be guarded a bit more. It's particularly helpful to have a machine that's out in the open on the Internet and not behind some sort of protective device. You can only select ports and protocols to allow access; that is, you cannot selectively deny or configure stateful filtering, or do anything else. In fact, in future versions of Windows, the user interface for this function will be greatly improved. It allows you to select common services that a machine may be running and selectively allow them access, rather than having to come up with the entire list of ports you wish to allow without any assistance from Windows.

Protecting Against Viruses

CMP's *TechEncyclopedia* defines viruses as "software used to infect a computer." And infect certainly is a word with multiple implications. In the past, viruses wreaked all sorts of havoc, from displaying a large image of a cannabis leaf with a message urging governmental legalization of marijuana to killing the boot sector on a computer's hard disk, thereby rendering it unbootable. Some even destroyed data. But most viruses were limited to the recipient's system and the only way for them to spread was through floppy disks and other removable, writable media.

A consequence of today's well-connected society, however, is the prevalence of Internet worms, Trojan horses, and other assorted nasties that currently plague our IT assets. As I write this, the Microsoft Blaster worm is spreading itself around the Internet, infecting countless computers with little or no protection. As an administrator, you must be vigilant at counteracting the threat posed by viruses. Consider the following tips:

- Subscribe to virus-related mailing lists. NTBuqTraq (http://www.ntbugtraq .com) is perhaps the most venerable of these lists, but any major antivirus product vendor will have these lists available and open to the public. Actively skimming the posts to these lists provides you with a leg up on the competition, because warnings and acknowledgments of new virus threats typically pass through those mediums before a general infection begins.

- Purchase antivirus software specifically designed for NT. Most consumer or prosumer antivirus products aren't designed for NT's environment, which hampers a lot of the low-level operating-system access these programs need. Make sure that you buy only software designed for Windows NT systems.

- Configure your antivirus software to perform automatic virus-definition updates. These are generally free for one year with the purchase of an antivirus package, and even the renewal fees are a small price to pay compared to the cost of a rampant infection.

- Pay considerable attention to the integrity of code and applications downloaded from the Internet. Something from the Internet may not be what it seems, and that particular scenario is becoming more likely with each day. Test downloaded code in a "sandboxed" system, that is, unconnected to the Internet, in order to ensure that it has no malicious intent or effects.

- Install software as a un- or under-privileged user. Try to avoid software that requires administrator privileges to run. Always generate a new user account for a new software package that you don't necessarily trust. Grant it just enough rights and permissions for the program to run.

Assigning Rights to Users

In conjunction with system policies, user rights serve to define the boundaries of acceptable actions on the parts of users of a Windows NT system. User rights take a broader view, and generally aren't concerned so much with any single action, but with a "genre" of actions that affect system behavior as a whole. User rights also tend to be limited to classes of users below administrators. That is to say, with few exceptions, members of the Administrators group are never prevented from performing tasks vital to their daily duties no matter what a user-rights setting might indicate.

There are two fundamental groups of rights: basic and advanced. Basic rights are those commonly assigned to users and groups and those that typically might be reassigned and otherwise altered from their default. Advanced rights are those that sparingly need to be changed from their default settings. In addition, advanced rights are mainly granted to applications and administrators, not lower-level regular users and power users.

Granting and Revoking User Rights

User rights are assigned from within the User Manager (or User Manager for Domains). Click the Policies menu, and then select User Rights. This opens a User Rights Policy box, which specifies the domain or computer to which the rights settings will apply. You can also see the specific right, which can be changed using the drop-down list, as well as the list of users to which the right is granted. You can enable the display of advanced rights, as described earlier in this section, by checking the appropriate box at the bottom of the window.

Table 2-4 lists all user rights available to be defined, their function, and the recommended users and groups that should be granted that right. Generally, from an ease-of-management standpoint, it's best to grant rights to groups of users rather than individual users. By granting individual rights you'll find yourself in a patchwork of differing permissions among users. This will make it difficult to track and troubleshoot access problems. In addition, the default groups to which Windows NT assigns rights are already in a reasonably hardened rights structure. You shouldn't find much need to change the groups or the rights.

Table 2-4. All User Rights Assignable in Windows NT

RIGHT	GROUP	FUNCTION	RECOMMENDED GROUPS TO GRANT RIGHT
Access this computer from a network	Basic	Allows access to shared resources to external computers	Everyone
Add workstations to domain	Basic	Introduces a new machine to a specific security domain	Administrators
Back up files and directories	Basic	Accesses files independent of their ACLs for the purposes of backing them up	Administrators, backup operators, server operators
Change the system time	Basic	Changes the system's internal clock	Administrators, server operators
Forces shutdown from a remote system	Basic	Shuts down a remote server	Administrators
Load and unload device drivers	Basic	Removes and installs device drivers on their respective removal or insertion	Administrators
Log on locally	Basic	Logs on at the system console	Administrators, server operators, backup operators, print operators, account operators, (for workstations) Everyone
Manage auditing and security log	Basic	Configures objects to be audited and the schedule for those audits	Administrators
Restore files and directories	Basic	Accesses files independent of their ACLs for the purposes of restoring them from a backup	Administrators, backup operators, server operators

Table 2-4. All User Rights Assignable in Windows NT (Continued)

RIGHT	GROUP	FUNCTION	RECOMMENDED GROUPS TO GRANT RIGHT
Shut down the system	Basic	Shuts down the system when logged on at the console	Administrators, server operators
Take ownership of files or other objects	Basic	Seizes ownership of a file or folder independent of its configured permissions	Administrators
Act as part of the operating system	Advanced	Runs with system permissions (which is essentially unfiltered access to everything)	None
Bypass traverse checking	Advanced	Accesses a file regardless of permissions of its upper-level folders	Everyone
Create a page file	Advanced	Constructs and configures a paging file for virtual memory	Administrators
Create a token object	Advanced	Makes a token	None
Create permanent shared objects	Advanced	Makes objects that programs and the operating system can share	None
Debug programs	Advanced	Runs with debug bits configured for access	Administrators
Generate security audits	Advanced	Sets audit events according to a system audit policy	None
Increase quotas	Advanced	Modifies system-resource heap quotas and controls access to memory and CPU time	Administrators

Table 2-4. All User Rights Assignable in Windows NT (Continued)

RIGHT	GROUP	FUNCTION	RECOMMENDED GROUPS TO GRANT RIGHT
Increase scheduling priority	Advanced	Raises the priority of a process against all other running processes	Administrators
Lock pages in memory	Advanced	Restrains a page of data to real memory for an indefinite period of time	None
Log on as a batch job	Advanced	Used for applications that can register as a batch with the operating system	None
Log on as a service	Advanced	Used for applications that can register as a service with the operating system	None
Modify firmware environment values	Advanced	Hardware-dependent modification of variables regarding a session	Administrators
Profile single process	Advanced	Takes statistics on process performance for one specific process	Administrators
Profile system performance	Advanced	Uses the Performance Monitor utility	Administrators
Replace a process-level token	Advanced	Modifies a process's environment	None

Checkpoints

In this chapter, I've discussed complete solutions for hardening an NT system against several different kinds and methods of attack. Briefly, the main action points are as follows:

- Use Windows NT System Policies and the System Policy Editor to set appropriately restrictive system policies for your organization.

- Set the maximum password age for your users to 90 days.

- Set the minimum password age for your users to 1 day.

- Set the minimum password length for your users to eight characters.

- Set the uniqueness factor for your passwords to at least five.

- Set the account lockout settings to five failed attempts and a counter reset after ten minutes.

- Change your NT/2000/XP passwords that contain only numbers and letters so that they also include at least one other nonalphanumeric character.

- Rename the administrator account carefully.

- Remove the Everyone group from the ACLs and add the Authenticated Users group in its place.

- Disable the Guest account.

- Disable remote access and control of the Registry, or at the very minimum tightly control it.

- Disable the display of the username of the last person to have used the system.

- Set tight permissions on the security event log.

- Set tight permissions on printers and printer drivers, particularly those associated with certain sensitive roles, such as invoicing and check production.

- Disable anonymous logins, particularly their ability to list account names.

- Set tight permissions on the ability to set scheduled tasks, either via the Windows GUI or through the command-line AT tool.

- Secure local directories and assign restrictive permission to the Everyone or Authenticated Users group on those directories.

- Ensure that system directories come before anything else in the search path.

- Lock down the operating-system directory very securely.

- Use the included port-filtering utility to restrict network traffic to incoming ports on which legitimate business is conducted.

- Be aware of new threats by subscribing to virus-related mailing lists.

- Purchase antivirus software specifically designed for NT, not just any software for "all versions of Windows."

- Configure your antivirus software to perform automatic virus-definition updates, preferably on a nightly or at least weekly basis.

- Pay considerable attention to the integrity of code and applications downloaded from the Internet.

- Install software as an un- or under-privileged user.

- Grant user rights only to those users who need it.

- Assign default user rights to appropriate groups, as detailed earlier in the chapter.

CHAPTER 3

Windows 2000 Security

WINDOWS SUFFERS FROM THE **WOOB** syndrome: It's wide open out of the box so that the user has all features and capabilities accessible to him automatically if he wants them. Unfortunately, the undesirables on the Internet have decided to take advantage of this unguarded default state and use it as a basis for staging attacks, hack attempts, and general computing mayhem.

This chapter focuses on protecting a Windows 2000 Professional and Server, Windows XP Professional, and Windows Server 2003 through the use of system updates and update audits, password policies, user-account protection, and basic local computer-security policies.

System Updates

The first step to configuring any new Windows system is to update it with the latest service pack. Service packs are updates to critical Windows system files based on bug reports, security vulnerabilities, and (rarely) new features. Windows operating system service packs are normally cumulative, in that they contain all fixes and service packs previous to the current level.

As of this writing, the latest pack level available for the Windows 2000 platform is Service Pack 4. The Windows XP client platform also has Service Pack 1 available. Both of these update packs are offered in two distinct versions:

- **Windows Update service:** With this option, the Windows Update website downloads an ActiveX control to your computer and searches your installed operating system for updates that are needed. It then custom-delivers a service pack to you based on the update level of your current system. For example, you may have downloaded five of nine critical security updates. The version of the service pack you receive will be built to deliver the remaining four updates and anything else that hasn't already been updated. Surf to http://www.windowsupdate.com to get started using this version.

- **Network Download version**. This is the complete service pack executable file designed to be stored on a file server and installed from a central location, either manually by a system administrator or automatically using automated tools like Systems Management Server or Microsoft Operations Manager. These files are usually hundreds of megabytes in size, so they're apt to be burned on CD and stored for easy distribution. The network download version of Windows 2000 Service Pack 3 is available from `http://download.microsoft.com/download/win2000platform/SP/SP3/NT5/EN-US/W2Ksp3.exe`. The network download version of Windows XP Service Pack 1 is available from `http://download.microsoft.com/download/whistler/SP/SP1/WXP/en-us/xpsp1_en_x86.exe`.

The "Slipstreaming" Process

Many administrators complain that as they receive new systems to deploy on the corporate network, it takes an increasing amount of time, relative to the age of the operating system (and therefore the number and complexity of updates released for that OS) to get said systems prepared for everyday usage. Even if the systems come with an operating system preinstalled and updated, it's likely that you have your own way of initially configuring a system and its applications, and you probably wipe the system clean and reinstall the system.

You may have an image file to aid in new system deployment, created using a tool like Symantec's Ghost or the Altiris line of network management and deployment tools, but you still must keep your master image updated. Hence, a real need is created for a standard Windows distribution CD-ROM with the latest service pack completely integrated, or "slipstreamed."

Fortunately, Microsoft has made it easy to create this handy tool. You'll need the network/administrative (in other words, the full) version of the service pack for your respective platform. To create the slipstreamed CD do the following:

1. Copy a stock Windows distribution CD into a directory on your hard drive. For the remainder of this example, let's use c:\windist. You'll likely need to create this directory.

2. Create a directory called c:\winsp, and copy the downloaded service pack file there. Let's assume the service pack file is named w2ksp3.exe.

3. Extract the service pack to that directory by executing the following command from the command line or by selecting Start ➤ Run: w2ksp3.exe –x.

4. Now, update the files from the regular Windows distribution CD with the new service pack files by executing the following command from the command line or from Start ➤ Run: D:\win2ksp3\i386\UPDATE\ UPDATE.EXE -S:C:\windist.

The files are then updated, and the process is complete. At this point, you can create a new CD for your own purposes, or create an administrative share for use with Remote Installation Service (RIS) and other tools. Slipstreaming is an easy way to make sure new systems are updated before they're ever put into production.

Critical Updates and Security Hotfixes

Of course, it takes time to create service packs and test them for wide distribution. And it seems new bugs and security vulnerabilities are discovered on a daily basis, if not more often. To address these problems, Microsoft releases "hotfixes," which patch specific problems. Normally, these aren't as widely tested as service packs, which have formal technical beta programs with thousands of testers with various systems and implementations, and they sometimes can cause instability. However, a cogent risk versus reward analysis would generally lead a prudent administrator to believe that applying hotfixes is a good protective measure.

There are a couple of different ways to get your systems updated with the latest hotfix files. As described earlier in this chapter, you can visit Windows Update (http://www.windowsupdate.com) and dynamically receive any updates that Microsoft deems important. Also, with Windows 2000 Service Pack 3 and all versions of Windows XP Home and Professional, the Critical Update Notification (CUN) service is available. This tool periodically checks the Windows Update catalog for new updates and alerts you to their presence. Upon installation of either the service pack or Windows XP itself, you should be prompted to configure this service.

Managing Critical Updates Across Multiple Computers

While the CUN tool and Windows Update are nice for individual users and small organizations, there is a more appropriate tool for network administrators. Microsoft has licensed a utility from Shavlik Technologies called HFNetChk. HFNetChk is a command-line tool that scans client computers for installed updates and patches. The comparison is based on an XML file of all available updates and the criteria for those updates, and Microsoft constantly updates the list.

The first time you run the tool, the tool will download the signed XML file, verify its authenticity, and decompress the file. HFNetChk then scans the selected computers to figure out the level of the operating system, service packs, and programs installed on the systems. HFNetChk looks at three aspects of your system to determine if a patch is installed: the Registry key that's installed by the patch, the file version, and the checksum for each file that's installed by the patch. By default, HFNetChk compares the files and Registry details on the computer that's being scanned to the XML file it downloads. If any of the three criteria discussed previously aren't satisfied, the tool considers the associated patch to be absent, and the results are displayed on the console. In the default configuration, HFNetChk output displays only those patches that are necessary to bring your computer up to date.

To use the tool, enter and run **hfnetchk** from the command line. Table 3-1 lists some command-line switches and their use.

Table 3-1. Basic HFNetChk Command-Line Switches

SWITCH	FUNCTION
-h	Specifies the NetBIOS computer name to scan. Separate multiple host names with a comma. Example: hfnetchk -h computer1, computer2, server1, server2
-fh	Specifies the name of a file that contains NetBIOS computer names to scan, with one computer name on every line and up to 256 listings in the file. Example: hfnetchk -fh computers_to_scan.txt
-i	Specifies the Internet Protocol (IP) address of the computer to scan. Separate multiple IP addresses with a comma. Example: hfnetchk -i 172.16.1.10, 172.16.1.50, 192.168.1.10
-fip	Specifies the name of a file that contains addresses to scan, with one IP address for every line and up to 256 listings in a file. Example: hfnetchk -fip IP_addresses_to_scan.txt
-r	Specifies the IP address range to be scanned, starting with ipaddress1 and ending with ipaddress2 inclusive. Example: hfnetchk -r 172.16.1.1-172.16.1.35
-d	Specifies that all computers in the NetBIOS domain name should be scanned. Example: hfnetchk -d
-n	Scans all computers available on the network.
-b	Scans only for those hotfixes marked as baseline critical by Microsoft. This switch requires the latest service pack to be installed.

Table 3-1. Basic HFNetChk Command-Line Switches (Continued)

SWITCH	FUNCTION
-o	Specifies the desired output format. "tab" outputs in tab-delimited format, which is useful for importing results into spreadsheets or databases. "wrap" outputs in a word-wrapped format. Example: hfnetchk -o tab
-x	Specifies the XML data source that contains the hotfix information. The location may be an XML file name, compressed XML .cab file, or a Uniform Resource Locator (URL). Example: hfnetchk -x mssecure.xml

Security Templates

Microsoft wisely decided to ship Windows 2000 with a few predefined security settings files, hereafter referred to as "security templates." These files contain what are essentially recipes for configuring a machine's security policy based on its daily role. There are six predefined security templates:

- For computers running Windows 2000 Professional, basicwk.inf and securewk.inf

- For computers running Windows 2000 Server, basicsv.inf and securesv.inf

- For computers running Windows 2000 Server and functioning as a domain controller, basicdc.inf and securedc.inf

Inside these templates are specifications for almost all aspects of local security policy—the only area of local policy not included is user rights and groups. You'll need to configure any desired user rights and groups modifications yourself. Additionally, Microsoft chose to include incremental security templates that go above and beyond the specifications made in the basic templates. These templates, designed to be applied to new Windows 2000 installations that have already had a basic template applied, must be used on systems formatted with NTFS, at least on the boot partition (the one containing the operating system files). The incremental security templates are as follows:

- For workstations or servers in which users ought to be prevented from being in the Power Users group, apply the compatws.inf template. This template compensates for the lack of additional privileges afforded to members of the Power Users group by relaxing the rights restrictions on the normal Users group.

- To further secure workstations or servers, the securews.inf template increases the overall security level of a machine by tightening areas of the OS not under the purview of rights and restrictions. Areas that are more secured using this template include account policy settings, auditing controls, and Registry keys that are prominent in security policy. The appropriate version of this template for Windows 2000 domain controllers is securedc.inf.

- For the ultraparanoid and those with the most stringent security requirements, the hisecws.inf file (and for domain controllers, the hisecdc.inf file) can be used; however, because all network transmissions must be signed and encrypted by Windows 2000 machines, this template is appropriate only in pure Windows 2000 or greater environments.

These convenient templates are designed to be used with the Security Templates snap-in to the Microsoft Management Console (MMC). Using the snap-in, you can apply the basic and incremental security templates included with the product, or you can make custom modifications to the templates and create your own easily distributable template.

To begin using the Security Templates snap-in, follow this procedure:

1. Enter and run **mmc /s** from a command line. This loads the Microsoft Management Console in author mode, allowing you to add a snap-in.

2. From the Console menu, select Add/Remove Snap-in. Then select Add. This opens a dialog box titled Add Standalone Snap-in.

3. From the list, select Security Templates, click Add, and then click Close.

4. Click OK in the next dialog box to confirm the addition of the snap-in.

You now have the Security Templates snap-in added to a console. From this snap-in, you can expand the Security Templates section in the console tree on the left, and then expand the C:\WINNT\security\templates folder to view the predefined security templates that were previously discussed.

Creating a Custom Security Template

You may wish to make your own customized policy modifications that go above and beyond those made in the templates shipped with Windows 2000. Creating a custom security template affords you an easy way to package, deploy, and apply these modifications with minimal administrative headaches. Best of all, you can use these templates in conjunction with a utility called the Security

Configuration and Analysis tool to assess the overall "hardness," or state of security, of your machines.

To create your own security template, do the following:

1. In the Security Templates console, expand Security Templates in the tree view on the left, and right-click C:\WINNT\security\templates (this is the default templates folder in the system).

2. Select New Template from the context menu that appears.

You may now make any policy modifications you wish in any one of the policy areas supported by the tool: account policies, local policies, the event log, restricted groups, system services, the Registry, and the file system. Your additions, deletions, and other changes are saved directly into the template as they're made.

To take this one step further, you may decide to build on the basic policy settings provided by the basic and incremental templates shipped with Windows 2000. In that case, it's quite simple to open the basic or incremental templates, resave to a different name, and make further modifications to it in order to create your own custom template, as shown in the following procedure:

1. Select an existing template inside the Security Templates console. In this example, I'll use the securews.inf file.

2. Right-click the existing template, and choose Save As from the context menu.

3. Give the new template a name, as shown in Figure 3-1.

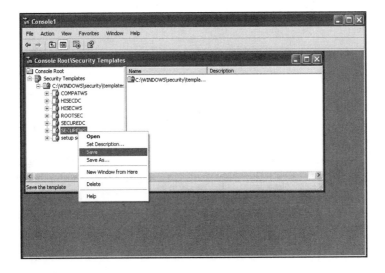

Figure 3-1. Creating a new security template

4. Click OK. The new template is created with the settings from the old basic template.

Recommended Security Policy Settings

In the following subsections, I'll discuss the security-policy settings that I recommend for a hardened Windows 2000 installation, regardless of whether you use the predefined security templates covered earlier in the chapter or not. I've broken these down into two sections: user accounts that cover ways to harden multiuser environments against attacks from both the outside and the inside, and local options, which give you ways to configure the operating system to protect itself against data hijacking, hacked transmissions, and unauthorized logons.

User Accounts

Multiuser systems are security holes in and of themselves. If you recall, the Windows NT operating system achieved government C2-level (orange book) security accreditation back in the mid-1990s. Although this seemed impressive initially, the joke was that the OS was only C2-certifiable in a nonnetworked, standalone environment. Given that NT was billed as a network operating system that would be used by many people, it was effectively a nonstarter to use C2 as a selling point.

Unfortunately, everyone needs multiple user accounts, so this section focuses on hardening these accounts as much as possible.

Password Requirements

Long passwords are more secure, period. The mathematics of the issue are fairly obvious: There are more permutations and combinations to try when brute-force cracking a longer password. Additionally, common English words (on which a dictionary attack can be based) are usually shorter than eight characters, making them easy to crack. Finally, aging passwords are insecure. Though most users tend to change their passwords on a regular basis when encouraged by administrators, some accounts—namely the Administrator and Guest accounts—often have the same password for life, which makes them an easy target for attack. To set these restrictions, do the following:

1. Open the Microsoft Management Console and navigate to the Local Computer Policy snap-in. This is normally under Start ➤ Programs ➤ Administrative Tools.

2. Navigate down the tree, through Security Settings, to Account Policies.

3. Click Password Policy.

4. Enable the Passwords Must Meet Complexity Requirements setting.

5. Change the Minimum Password Length to 8 characters.

6. Change the Maximum Password Age setting to 90 days.

Account Lockout Policies

An old-fashioned method for gaining unauthorized access to a system is to attempt authentication using a known username, or an unknown username that's derived logically along with a different password on each attempt. Windows can thwart this attack using an account lockout policy, which will disable an account for a specified period of time after a certain number of unsuccessful logon attempts.

To set the account lockout policy, do the following:

1. Open the Microsoft Management Console and navigate to the Local Computer Policy snap-in. This is normally under Start ➤ Programs ➤ Administrative Tools.

2. Navigate down the tree, through Security Settings, to Account Policies.

3. Click Account Lockout Policy.

4. Set the Account Lockout Threshold to 3 for the maximum number of bad login attempts.

5. Set both the Account Lockout Duration and Reset Account Lockout After options to 15 minutes.

Local Options

In addition to securing local accounts, the newer Windows platforms give you the ability to lock down certain rights and configurations on the local computer, beyond any domain security policy that might be configured. Several of the options available do little to thwart attacks, so in this section I've covered the seven most effective changes you can make to your local security policy.

 NOTE *You can enable all of the hardening suggestions in this section in the Security Options section of the Microsoft Management Console's Local Computer Policy snap-in. You can find this snap-in normally by selecting Start ➤ Programs ➤ Administrative Tools. To get to the appropriate section, navigate to the snap-in tree by selecting Computer Configuration ➤ Windows Settings ➤ Security Settings ➤ Local Policies. Then click Security Options, and the different configuration switches will appear in the right-hand pane.*

The instructions in this section assume that you've already loaded the snap-in and navigated to the appropriate section.

Anonymous Access

Windows allows access by an anonymous user to many shares and files through the use of a null user account; this is a security hazard, of course. You can still enable anonymous access to files and directories by explicitly granting rights to the ANONYMOUS USER account in Windows inside the appropriate access control list (ACL). This setting merely disables it by default, so you know exactly where connections are being made.

To fix this hazard, set the Additional Restrictions for Anonymous Connections selection to No Access Without Explicit Anonymous Permissions.

Shut Down Without Logon

Windows 2000 and Windows XP Professional machines come in a default configuration that allows you to shut down the system through the use of the Shutdown button on the logon screen. Windows 2000 and .NET servers disable this out of the box. Despite the convenience factor that this feature affords, it's best to leave rebooting a machine to an aware user.

Disable the Allow System to Shut Down Without Having to Log On selection to secure this.

Automatic Logoff

Some users log on to the network and then don't log off for months. This is a prominent security hole, because when that user leaves her desk, she is still authenticated to the network with her credentials. These can be used to do destructive things: file deletion and transfer, planting of a "root kit" or backdoor program, or password changing.

The way to make this work is twofold: First, each valid user needs to have a time when he isn't permitted to log on. This can be somewhere in the morning for a standard 9 AM to 5 PM office, perhaps at 3 AM to 3:30 AM. Then, you need to make a change to the local security policy so that when the user's logon time expires, he isn't permitted to log on.

To set up a logon time restriction on a domain controller for an Active Directory–enabled domain, do the following:

1. Go to the Active Directory Users & Computers snap-in.

2. Expand the icon for your domain, and click the Users container.

3. Right-click a username, and select Properties.

4. Click the Account tab, and then click the Logon Hours button.

5. Select the appropriate region of time in the calendar block, and click the radio buttons to the right to either permit or deny logons during that time.

6. Click OK once, and then again to exit the user property sheet.

This option is only available on Active Directory–enabled machines.

Now, make the change to the computer's local security policy. In the Local Computer Policy snap-in, enable the Automatically Log Off Users When Logon Time Expires option. If you don't have a domain, you should enable the Automatically Log Off Users When Logon Time Expires (local) option.

Digitally Signing Communication

It's a good idea these days for a computer to authenticate itself to other computers during a communication. Otherwise, a technique called "spoofing" could be used, and a cracker's computer could pose as the remote end of a connection and acquire potentially sensitive information. You can prevent this by using digital signatures. However, they aren't pervasive; Windows compensates for this limited use by providing two options in the local policy: require them when possible, or require them, period.

I recommend requiring the signatures when possible on both ends of a connection (the remote procedure call, or RPC) protocol refers to the requesting end as the "client" and the responding end as the "server," no matter the systems' usual roles). Unsigned transmissions should only occur when signatures aren't available, supported, or possible.

To require digitally signed communication when possible, enable the Digitally Sign Client Communication (When Possible) and Digitally Sign Server Communication (When Possible) options.

Requiring the Three-Keystroke Salute at Logon

The logon screen is one of the most trusted aspects of a computer to a normal user. She trusts it enough that she gives her password and username, and then the computer trusts her, too, if all of that is correct and verified. A cracker can take advantage of this mutual trust by writing a program that runs as a system service—that is, it doesn't need user privileges. The program will mimic the logon box, grab the user's input, and do something with it. "It" could be emailing the password to the cracker, saving the credentials to a backdoor program data file, or any number of other nefarious things. However, pressing Ctrl-Alt-Del brings Windows itself to attention, and you get the authentic Windows logon instead of a shell of one that a cracker creates. This is an easy step that makes your system much more secure.

To require this keystroke, disable the Disable Ctrl-Alt-Del Requirement for Logon option. (Yes, that's right. Microsoft uses some questionable terminology.)

Last Username Display

By default, Windows displays the username of the last successfully authenticated person who used that particular system on the logon screen. This is giving needless information away, although some of your users are probably accustomed to it.

To disable the last username from being displayed, enable the Do Not Display Last User Name in Logon Screen option.

Password Expiration Prompt

Earlier in this chapter I discussed setting password policies to prevent brute-force attacks. Of course, changing passwords is a problem for some users, who'd rather not be bothered with Internet security (IS) minutia and would like to simply use their computers to be productive. With this policy setting, you can tell the system to automatically remind a user when his password will expire and prompt him to change it. Setting this value to 14 days gives a user ample opportunity to change his password, because that's in excess of most scheduled vacations and business trips.

To enable the password expiration prompt, set the Prompt User to Change Password Before Expiration option to 14 Days at Minimum.

Other Security Considerations

Although the earlier sections discussed policy modifications that will harden a Windows 2000 installation, there are other facets of the operating system that do require attention. Although simply making the policy modifications takes you partially on the journey to a hardened system, it's only a portion of the full process. This section presents some areas that deserve your consideration.

Windows Component Selection and Installation

Security is a minimalist attitude: That is to say, when you harden a system, you want as few basic entry points as possible. This in effect shortens the length of the playing field for an intruder: She has fewer processes and fewer software products whose flaws she can exploit, and there's less chance that you, the administrator, will configure something improperly or forget it entirely. Windows 2000 makes this a little more difficult, especially at install time, when it isn't possible to select components that you would like *not* to be installed.

If I might offer a slight editorial aside, this is a serious flaw in Windows and a HUGE mistake on Microsoft's part. It would have been bad enough if Microsoft decided that none of their operating systems should ever present the user with component installation options. But this functionality remains available in the Windows 9x line and even in Windows NT! And yet mysteriously, it isn't present in Windows 2000 or Server 2003. It's baffling to me why these options were removed at the point of installation. If anyone from Microsoft is reading this, please return the power of choice to me, the user!

Tightening Running Services

Continuing with the minimalist approach, you need to ensure that the only services or processes running on your system are those that (a) you know about and (b) are critical to the functioning of a particular system or resource. This seems like a simple task initially, but Microsoft has made life a bit more difficult than it should be by failing to properly document which services are dependent on others. Therefore, it's foolhardy to open the Services console and simply begin turning off services at random, hoping to tighten the network through broad, sweeping motions. It just won't work. Instead, peruse the following list, making note of the bare minimum of services required to run Windows 2000:

- DNS Client

- Event Log

- File Replication (only on a domain controller)

- Kerberos Key Distribution Center (only on a domain controller)

- Logical Disk Manager

- Net Logon (only on a domain controller)

- NT LM Service Provider (only on a domain controller)

- Plug & Play

- Protected Storage

- RPC Locator (only on a domain controller)

- Security Accounts Manager

- Server (only on machines hosting resources to be shared)

- Windows Time (only on a domain controller)

- Workstation (only on machines connecting to other machines' shared resources)

Checkpoints

In this chapter, I've discussed updating your Windows 2000, XP, or .NET machine to the latest levels available and securing your system through password, account, and computer policies. Use the following quick-reference checkpoints to ensure that you've covered each step in the chapter appropriately.

- Update to the latest service-pack level for your platform.

- Create a "slipstreamed" distribution CD to deploy the latest service-pack update to any new OS installs.

- Use the latest hotfix file patches from Microsoft to relieve your system of vulnerabilities.

- Download and use HFNetChk to scan and inventory your network for security-patch installations.

- Set restrictions on Windows passwords. They should be at least six characters long, they shouldn't be based on a dictionary word, and they shouldn't last longer than 90 days.

- Configure Windows to disable or "lock out" accounts for at least 15 minutes after three unsuccessful authentication attempts.

- Disable all anonymous access except where explicitly allowed in file-system permissions.

- Disable the ability to shut down a system without first logging in to it.

- Enable automatic logoff upon logon time expiration, and set up at least one half hour each night during which no user is permitted to log on.

- Require digitally signed communications when possible, but not always.

- Require the user to press Ctrl-Alt-Del before logging on, a key sequence recognized only by the Windows operating system.

- Do not permit the username of the last user to be displayed at logon.

- Remind users to change their password automatically at least 14 days before its expiration.

CHAPTER 4

Windows XP Security

THE ADVENT OF ALWAYS-ON connections and the increase of business connectivity to the Internet has resulted in Windows XP computers being directly connected to the Internet, which is a hotbed of potentially dangerous people and computers. In this chapter, you'll look at ways to specifically protect your Windows XP computers from threats that reside abroad.

Implementing a Firewall

It's simply a given that on Windows XP, you should install a firewall. If you have a case of the cheaps, you should use the included Internet Connection Firewall (ICF) to control access to services running on the machine. It's a simple process to configure the ICF, and by doing so you harden the exterior interfaces to the machine from public access.

To configure the ICF, do the following:

1. Open Control Panel, and double-click Network Connections.

2. Double-click the connection that refers to your external interface. The connection status window appears.

3. Click the Properties button.

4. Navigate to the Advanced tab, and select the box titled Protect My Computer and Network by Limiting or Preventing Access to This Computer from the Internet.

5. Click OK.

Your computer is now protected by the ICF. You can also click the Settings button on the Advanced tab to open specific ports for certain services you might be running.

You should also enable ICF logging on critical computers directly connected to the Internet. Doing so will provide you with an audit trail for later forensic analysis; you can automatically see what changes a hacker or cracker may have made to your system so you can reverse them efficiently. To enable logging, navigate to the Security Logging tab in the Advanced Settings dialog box, as shown in Figure 4-1.

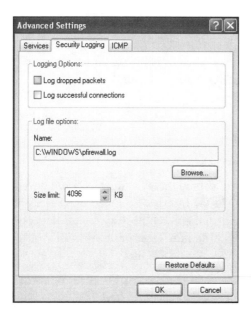

Figure 4-1. Enabling ICF security logging

You can choose whether to log successful connections and packets that are dropped because of firewall rules, and you can also specify a custom location for the log file itself.

TIP *Another reason to upgrade to XP: NT 4 is nearing the end of its life. Users should plan an upgrade to Windows XP or 2003. Users of Windows 2000 Desktop should consider an upgrade to Windows XP if only for the ICF filtering provided.*

If you have a small business or home business network connected to the Internet, the most cost-effective way to obtain the most protection possible for your dollar is to purchase a broadband router, such as those manufactured by Linksys, D-Link, NETGEAR, and others. Most of these units even have built-in switches, and you simply connect each client to the router and the computers are automatically protected—by default—from the outside. Of course, this strategy won't be as effective when your computing base grows, but it's an efficient solution for a small business or home business.

Changes to Services

One of the easiest ways for crackers to exploit holes in your system is through open services. In addition to the security benefits you get from auditing and closing unused services, you also receive a performance enhancement because stagnant programs aren't taking up available resources. Besides, a full security audit of your service can reveal some interesting details about your machine. Lately, viruses have been masquerading as services listed in the Task Manager, making them harder to detect, clean, and prevent.

Windows XP comes with only a few services that really require open access to an external interface for normal operation: Terminal Services, or Remote Desktop Connection, and the Remote Access Service for answering dial-in calls.

To manage services on your computer, do the following:

1. Right-click My Computer, and choose Manage.

2. Expand the Services & Applications tab, and select Services.

3. Double-click a service.

4. Under Startup Type select Manual to disable a service from automatically starting upon computer bootup. Click the Stop button to stop the service if it's already running.

Table 4-1 contains a nearly complete list of all services that ship with Windows XP and the recommended state that each should be in on your computer, assuming normal office functions are being performed on the machine.

Table 4-1. Common Services and Recommended Settings

SERVICE NAME	DESCRIPTION	RECOMMENDED STATE
Alerter	Raises administrative alerts for selected users and computers.	Disabled.
Application Layer Gateway Service	Required if you use Internet Connection Sharing (ICS) or XP's included Internet Connection Firewall to connect to the Internet.	Automatic if using ICS; disabled if not.
Application Management	Used to assign, publish, and remove software through Group Policy.	Disabled unless you participate in an Active Directory domain.
Automatic Updates Services	Used to check if there are any critical updates available for download.	Requires Cryptographic to be running. Automatic if you don't wish to use Windows Update manually.
Background Intelligent Transfer Service	Used by Windows Update to transfer data in the background using otherwise idle available network bandwidth.	Disabled.
ClipBook	Enables the ClipBook Viewer to create and share data to be viewed by remote computers.	Disabled.
COM+ Event System	Provides automatic distribution of events to subscribing programmatic components.	Disabled.

Table 4-1. Common Services and Recommended Settings (Continued)

SERVICE NAME	DESCRIPTION	RECOMMENDED STATE
COM+ System Application	Provides automatic distribution of events to subscribing programmatic components.	Disabled.
Computer Browser	Maintains an up-to-date list of computers on your network, and supplies the list to programs that request it.	Disabled.
Cryptographic Services	Confirms signatures of Windows files. Required for Windows Update to function in manual and automatic mode, and required for Windows Media Player as well.	Automatic.
DHCP Client	Manages network configuration by registering and updating IP addresses and DNS server information.	Automatic if required; disabled if not.
Distributed Link Tracking Client	Maintains links between the NTFS file system files within a computer or across computers in a network domain.	Disabled.
Distributed Transaction Coordinator	Coordinates transactions that are distributed across multiple computer systems and/or resource managers, such as databases, message queues, file systems, or other transaction-protected resource managers.	Disabled.
DNS Client	Resolves and caches DNS names. The DNS client service must be running on every computer that will perform DNS name resolution.	Automatic.

Table 4-1. Common Services and Recommended Settings (Continued)

SERVICE NAME	DESCRIPTION	RECOMMENDED STATE
Error Reporting Service	Calls home to Microsoft when errors occur.	Disabled.
Event Log	Logs event messages issued by programs and Windows. This can be useful in diagnosing problems.	Automatic.
Fax Service	Enables you to send and receive faxes. Disabling this service will render the computer unable to send or receive faxes.	Disabled; or don't install from distribution media.
Telephony	Provides Java Telephony API (TAPI) support for programs that control telephony devices and IP-based voice connections on the local computer and through the LAN on servers that are also running the service.	Disabled unless required.
FTP Publishing Service	Not available on Windows XP Home. Not installed by default on Windows XP Pro. Enables FTP service.	Disabled; or don't install from distribution media.
Help and Support	Required for Microsoft's online help documents.	Automatic.
Human Interface Device Access	If all your devices function then disable it.	Disabled.
IIS Admin	Not available on Windows XP Home. Not installed by default on Windows XP Pro. Allows administration of Internet Information Services (IIS).	Disabled; or don't install from distribution media.
IMAPI CD-Burning COM Service	Used for the "drag-and-drop" CD-burn capability. You'll need this service to burn CDs.	Automatic.

Table 4-1. Common Services and Recommended Settings (Continued)

SERVICE NAME	DESCRIPTION	RECOMMENDED STATE
Indexing Service	Indexes contents and properties of files on local and remote computers and provides rapid access to files through a flexible querying language.	Disabled.
Internet Connection Firewall and Internet Connection Sharing	Provides network address translation (NAT), addressing and name resolution services for all computers on your home or small-office network through a dial-up or broadband connection.	Automatic if sharing connection, disabled if not required.
IPSEC Services	Manages IP security (IPsec) policy, starts the Internet Key Exchange (IKE), and coordinates IPsec policy settings with the IP security driver.	Disabled.
Logical Disk Manager	Watches Plug & Play events for new drives to be detected and passes volume and/or disk information to the Logical Disk Manager Administrative Service to be configured. If disabled, the Disk Management snap-in display will not change when disks are added or removed.	Manual.
Logical Disk Manager Administrative Service	See previous item's description.	Manual.

Table 4-1. Common Services and Recommended Settings (Continued)

SERVICE NAME	DESCRIPTION	RECOMMENDED STATE
Message Queuing	A messaging infrastructure and development tool for creating distributed messaging applications for Windows.	Disabled; or don't install from distribution media.
Message Queuing Triggers	Required only if you use Message Queuing Service.	Disabled; or don't install from distribution media.
Messenger	Sends and receives messages to or from users and computers, or those transmitted by administrators or by the Alerter Service.	Disabled.
MS Software Shadow Copy Provider	Used in conjunction with the Volume Shadow Copy Service. Microsoft Backup uses these services.	Enabled.
NetMeeting Remote Desktop Sharing	Allows authorized users to remotely access your Windows desktop from another PC over a corporate intranet by using NetMeeting.	Disabled.
Network Connections	Manages objects in the Network and Dial-Up Connections folder, in which you can view both network and remote connections.	Automatic.
Network DDE	Useless service unless you use remote ClipBook.	Disabled.
Network DDE DSDM	See previous item's description.	Disabled.

Table 4-1. Common Services and Recommended Settings (Continued)

SERVICE NAME	DESCRIPTION	RECOMMENDED STATE
Network Location Awareness (NLA)	Required for use with the Internet Connection Sharing Service (server only).	Disabled unless running ICS or ICF.
NTLM Security Support Provider	Enables users to log on to the network using the NTLM Authentication Protocol. If this service is stopped, users will be unable to log on to the domain and access services. NTLM is used mostly by Windows versions prior to Windows 2000.	Automatic.
Performance Logs and Alerts	Configures performance logs and alerts.	Disabled.
Plug & Play	Enables a computer to recognize and adapt to hardware changes with little or no user input.	Automatic.
Portable Media Serial Number	Retrieves serial numbers from portable music players connected to your computer.	Disabled.
Print Spooler	Queues and manages print jobs locally and remotely. If you don't have a printer attached, then disable.	Automatic.
Protected Storage	Provides protected storage for sensitive data, such as private keys, to prevent access by unauthorized services processes or users.	Disabled.
QoS RSVP	Provides network signaling and local, traffic-control functionality.	Disabled unless required by your network administrator.

Table 4-1. Common Services and Recommended Settings (Continued)

SERVICE NAME	DESCRIPTION	RECOMMENDED STATE
Remote Access Auto Connection Manager	Creates a connection to a remote network whenever a program references a remote DNS or NetBIOS name or address.	Disabled.
Remote Access Connection Manager	Creates a network connection.	Automatic if using Dial-Up Networking; disabled otherwise.
Remote Desktop Help Session Manager	Manages and controls Remote Assistance.	Disabled.
Remote Procedure Call (RPC)	Provides the endpoint mapper and other miscellaneous RPC services.	Automatic.
Remote Procedure Call Locator	Manages the RPC name service database.	Disabled.
Remote Registry Service	Not available on Windows XP Home. Allows users to connect to a remote registry and read and/or write keys to it—providing they have the required permissions.	Disabled.
Removable Storage	Manages removable media drives and libraries. This service maintains a catalog of identifying information for removable media used by a system, including tapes, CDs, and so on.	Disabled.
RIP Listener	Not installed by default.	Disabled; or don't install from distribution media.

Table 4-1. Common Services and Recommended Settings (Continued)

SERVICE NAME	DESCRIPTION	RECOMMENDED STATE
Routing and Remote Access	Offers routing services in local area and wide area network environments.	Disabled; or don't install from distribution media.
Secondary Logon	Allows you to run specific tools and programs with different permissions than your current logon provides.	Automatic.
Security Accounts Manager	Startup of this service signals other services that the Security Accounts Manager subsystem is ready to accept requests.	Automatic.
Server	Provides RPC support and file print and named pipe sharing over the network. The Server Service allows the sharing of your local resources (such as disks and printers) so that other users on the network can access them.	Automatic if you're sharing files; disabled if not.
Shell Hardware Detection	Used for the autoplay of devices like memory cards, some CD drives, and so on.	Disabled unless required.
Simple Mail Transport Protocol (SMTP)	Transports email across the network.	Disabled; or don't install from distribution media.
Simple TCP/IP Services	Implements support for a number of IP protocols.	Disabled; or don't install from distribution media.

Table 4-1. Common Services and Recommended Settings (Continued)

SERVICE NAME	DESCRIPTION	RECOMMENDED STATE
Smart Card	Manages and controls access to a smart card inserted into a smart card reader attached to the computer.	Disabled unless using a smart card reader.
Smart Card Helper	Provides support for earlier smart card readers attached to the computer.	Disabled unless using a smart card reader.
SNMP Service	Allows Simple Network Management Protocol (SNMP) requests to be serviced by the local computer.	Disabled; or don't install from distribution media.
SNMP Trap Service	Receives trap messages generated by local or remote SNMP agents and forwards the messages to SNMP management programs running on the computer.	Disabled; or don't install from distribution media.
SSDP Discovery Service	Used to locate UPnP devices on your home network.	Disabled.
System Event Notification	Tracks system events such as Windows logon network and power events.	Disabled.
System Restore Service	Creates system snapshots or restore points for returning to at a later time.	Disabled.
Task Scheduler	Enables a program to run at a designated time.	Disabled unless absolutely required.
TCP/IP NetBIOS Helper Service	Enables support for NetBIOS over TCP/IP (NetBT) service and NetBIOS name resolution. Only required if you need to share files with others.	Disabled unless sharing is enabled.

Table 4-1. Common Services and Recommended Settings (Continued)

SERVICE NAME	DESCRIPTION	RECOMMENDED STATE
TCP/IP Printer Server	Used for setting up a local UNIX print server.	Disabled; or don't install from distribution media.
Telephony	Provides Telephony API (TAPI) support for programs that control telephony devices and IP-based voice connections on the local computer and through the LAN on servers that are also running the service.	Disabled.
Telnet	Allows a remote user to log on to the system and run console programs by using the command line.	Disabled; or don't install from distribution media.
Terminal Services	Provides a multisession environment that allows client devices to access a virtual Windows 2000 Professional desktop session and Windows-based programs running on the server.	Disabled; or don't install from distribution media.
Themes	Used to display all those new XP themes and colors on your desktop. Lots of space needed.	Automatic or manual, depending on your preferences.
Uninterruptible Power Supply (UPS)	Manages communications with a UPS connected to the computer by a serial port.	Disabled unless using a UPS.
Universal Plug & Play Device Host	Used in conjunction with SSDP Discovery Service, it detects and configures UPnP devices on your home network.	Disabled.

Table 4-1. Common Services and Recommended Settings (Continued)

SERVICE NAME	DESCRIPTION	RECOMMENDED STATE
Upload Manager	As with BITS, this service manages file transfers between clients and servers on the network. This service is NOT required for basic File and Print sharing.	Disabled.
Volume Shadow Copy	Used in conjunction with the MS Software Shadow Copy Provider Service. Microsoft Backup uses these services.	Disabled.
WebClient	Disable this for security reasons.	Disabled.
Windows Audio	Used to produce audio.	Automatic.
Windows Image Acquisition (WIA)	Used for some scanners and cameras. If, after disabling this service, your scanner or camera fails to function properly, enable this service.	Disabled.
Windows Installer	Installs, repairs, or removes software according to instructions contained in MSI files provided with the applications.	Manual.
Windows Management Instrumentation (WMI)	Provides system management information. WMI is an infrastructure for building management applications and instrumentation shipped as an integral part of the current generation of Microsoft operating systems.	Automatic.

Table 4-1. Common Services and Recommended Settings (Continued)

SERVICE NAME	DESCRIPTION	RECOMMENDED STATE
Windows Management Instrumentation Driver Extension	Tracks all of the drivers that have registered WMI information to publish.	Manual.
Windows Time	Sets the computer clock. W32Time maintains date and time synchronization on all computers running on a Microsoft Windows network.	Automatic.
Wireless Zero Configuration	Automatic configuration for wireless network devices.	Disabled.
WMI Performance Adapter	Optimizes the speed of WMI queries.	Disabled.
Workstation	Provides network connections and communications. If this service is turned off, no network connections can be made to remote computers using Microsoft Networks.	Automatic.
World Wide Web Publishing Service	Provides HTTP services for applications on the Windows platform.	Disabled; or don't install from distribution media.

As you can see from the previous list, not very much is actually needed to keep your Windows XP installation functioning in a home environment. Most of the enabled services just pose an enormous security risk, bring little or no benefit, consume resources, and can be safely turned off.

Microsoft Baseline Security Analyzer Patch Check and Security Tests

Windows Update is a good way to update a few computers on your network, but it's a bad strategy for a large network because it requires user intervention and isn't easily automated. As you'll discover in Chapter 9, Microsoft has a better way to automate patch rollout on more than a handful of computers using their Software Update Services package. However, neither option offers a good, sweeping way of determining the update level of your machines.

To fill this need, Microsoft has issued the Baseline Security Analyzer (MBSA) tool, which will query each machine on your network and detect which available patches haven't been installed. The tool is simple to use, easy to automate, and is more suited to a mass analysis than Windows Update. However, it lacks the intelligence and logic of its web-based counterpart. You'll probably see a lot of updates that don't pertain to your machines, even though they aren't installed. It's up to you to verify that the specific patch listed in the results from the MBSA session doesn't apply to specific machines on your network. You'll also need to reboot after each patch application.

Installing Microsoft Baseline Security Analyzer

To install MBSA, follow this procedure:

1. Go to http://www.microsoft.com and search for hfnetchk. (I would include a link, but Microsoft has a tendency to change their website around quite often.)

2. Download, execute, and install the program to c:\hfnetchk.

3. At the command prompt, enter **hfnetchk –z –v.**

The –z and –v switches tell the MBSA tool to go out and download a database of all available patches. It will then scan a computer or set of computers for patches that haven't been installed, and indicate which haven't been installed along with the Microsoft Knowledge Base article number. You can look up the appropriate patch using the number provided by the MBSA at http://www.microsoft.com/support.

Penetration Tests

Many security vendors provide free or low-cost online tools that evaluate the security of your system, of course with the underlying motive of persuading you to buy their product. These tools are most often a "penetration test" that can indicate how effectively you've hardened your system.

Symantec offers their security check, as well as other tools, at `http://security.symantec.com`. Here you can scan for holes in your computer's external interfaces—a very basic penetration test—or scan for viruses that might be present on your system, and track a cracker's location if you have his source IP. If you've followed the steps in this chapter so far, I highly recommend taking advantage of the Scan for Security Risks option to ensure that you haven't missed anything. In addition to probing your open ports, the option can also detect some Trojan horse viruses that can invade your computer and open a back door.

There's one thing you should be aware of: Each of these Symantec tools download to your system Active X content, which of course should at least give a competent, astute administrator pause. It's up to you to trust a particular vendor. Generally, the more popular security-testing sites will have the most robust scanning tools.

Steve Gibson, of the venerable Gibson Research Corporation, has also made available the popular ShieldsUp! test, which is available at `http://www.grc.com`. It performs much the same function as the Symantec tools.

File System Security

Part of hardening your overall XP system is to ensure that your file system is adequately secured. Microsoft provides NT File System (NTFS) support in Windows XP. NTFS allows for more robust security features and user permissions and also adds some basic fault tolerance, with which the older FAT file system just cannot compete. Make sure all of your hard drives are formatted with NTFS unless you have systems that dual-boot to another, older operating system that doesn't support NTFS on the same disk.

To check your hard drive partitions, do the following:

1. Log in as Administrator, and double-click My Computer.

2. Right-click each hard drive letter and choose Properties.

3. Navigate to the General tab. Here, Windows will identify the file system type.

Follow the previous steps for each drive letter, noting which ones are labeled FAT or FAT32.

To convert a FAT or FAT32 partition to NTFS, do the following:

1. Open a command prompt.

2. At the command prompt, enter **convert *x:* /FS:NTFS /V**. Replace *x* with one of the drive letters you noted previously.

3. Repeat the previous step for each FAT or FAT32 partition.

When you're finished, reboot the system for the changes to take effect.

You might also choose to use third-party disk conversion utilities, like PartitionMagic or Norton Disk Doctor, to convert your file system to NTFS. It's a painless procedure, no matter which tool you use to do it. Of course, you should always remember to back up your data before performing any change to a disk's configuration or function.

Disable Automated Logins

Windows XP offers a feature for machines that aren't participating in a security domain where accounts without passwords can automatically log in at a computer's startup without requiring any user intervention. Obviously, this is a huge security hole for machines connected to any kind of network. You'll want to disable this.

To disable automated logins, do the following:

1. Inside Control Panel, open Administrative Tools.

2. Double-click Local Security Policy.

3. Select a username.

4. Make sure there is a password set for each user account that's enabled.

Hardening Default Accounts

The main premise is that in order for someone to access an XP system, she must have a username and password. To that effect, Windows creates the administrator account, for use by the machine's owner, and a Guest account, which has limited privileges and is designed for people who don't have continuing business on a machine. This isn't just an XP function.

Of course, crackers have taken advantage of the presence of both accounts. You might consider renaming the two accounts to reduce the surface vulnerability of the machine. This doesn't work for server machines all the time; sometimes server software and services require the administrator account to be named the same, but for client machines, renaming is usually a good strategy. This is true particularly for XP computers, because they tend to be directly connected to the Internet more than computers that are running older versions of Windows.

You can configure the Administrator account as follows:

1. Log in as Administrator.

2. Go to the Control Panel, double-click Administrative Tools, and then Computer Management.

3. Open Local Users and Groups.

4. Click the User folder.

5. Right-click the Administrator account, and choose to rename it. Make it a less obvious name.

6. Right-click this renamed Administrator account and select Set Password.

You can configure the Guest account as follows:

1. Right-click the Guest account, and choose to rename it. Make it a less obvious name.

2. Right-click this renamed Guest account, then select Set Password.

For security reasons, the Guest account in XP is disabled by default. Enabling the Guest account allows anonymous users to access the system. Even if no one sits down and logs in as a guest to your system, the account is used. If you share a folder, the default permission is that everyone has full control, and because Guest is included within the built-in Everyone group, a hole is opened. A standard practice is to always remove the share permissions from Everyone and add them to Authenticated Users. This is a much safer configuration.

Using Forensic Analysis Techniques

Part of hardening a system is knowing when your efforts haven't protected against or prevented an attack. Here are some common indicators that your system has been compromised:

- A system alert, alarm, or related indication from an intrusion-detection tool

- Suspicious entries in system or security logs in XP's Event Viewer

- Unsuccessful logon attempts

- New user accounts of unknown origin

- New files on the physical file system of unknown origin and function

- Unexplained changes or attempt to change file sizes, checksums, timestamps, especially on files within the C:\WINNT hierarchy

- Unexplained addition, deletion, or modification of data

- Denial of service activity or inability of one or more users to log in to an account, including admin or root logins to the console

- System crashes

- Poor system performance

- Unauthorized operation of a program or the addition of a sniffer application to capture network traffic or usernames or passwords

- Port scanning and the use of exploit and vulnerability scanners, remote requests for information about systems and users, or social-engineering attempts

- Unusual usage times; statistically, more security incidents occur during nonworking hours than any other time

- An indicated last time of usage for an account that doesn't correspond to the actual last time of usage for that account

- Unusual usage patterns; for example, programs are being compiled in the account of a user who doesn't know how to program

Keep alert for these indicators. If any are tripped, back up any personal data on a machine, verify that data's integrity, and then reformat the machine and reinstall Windows. It isn't a safe bet to try to reconstruct a compromised machine for later production use.

Checkpoints

If you're in a hurry, the action items within this chapter include the following:

- Use XP's included Internet Connection Firewall to close off open ports.

- Enable ICF logging for later forensic analysis and intrusion detection.

- If you have a small office or home office network, purchase an inexpensive broadband router for further protection.

- Adjust your running services list to match that in the book.

- Test your service load and ensure that only services required for necessary functionality are running and enabled.

- Use the Microsoft Baseline Security Analyzer (MBSA) to analyze the current update level of machines on your network.

- Also visit Windows Update to identify and install appropriate hotfixes and software updates.

- Visit a reputable online software vendor and perform penetration tests on your machines to ensure that ports are closed off and your hardening efforts were effective.

- Format the partitions on your machines with NTFS.

- Disable automated logins by ensuring there is a password for each user account on a machine. (This applies only to machines that aren't participating in a security domain.)

- Rename the Administrator account.

- Rename the Guest account.

- Replace the Everyone group with the Authenticated Users group inside the access control lists (ACLs) of your shares.

- Understand the typical signs of a compromised machine.

- If a machine becomes compromised, don't attempt to resurrect it. Get personal data off, verify the integrity of that data, and then reformat and reinstall the machine.

CHAPTER 5

Defining Enterprise Security Policies with Windows 2000 and Later

WINDOWS 2000 AND LATER operating systems come with an excellent, if a bit rocky, management system called Group Policy. Although the system drew a lot of criticism, namely from those opposed to Microsoft, there are a lot of positives to it.

Group Policy is a step in the right direction in many ways. For one, it somewhat assuages the need to purchase complex system management software like Microsoft Systems Management Server or IBM's Tivoli enterprise IT management products. Additionally, Group Policy offers Windows-specific management options that external products don't necessarily support (programmers familiar with Group Policy liken it to Windows NT's System Policy Editor on steroids). But Group Policy also functions as a rudimentary yet effective software advertisement and distribution mechanism. And finally, it provides Windows administrators with a way to centrally manage security configurations and permissions on client machines running Windows 2000 or later.

Group Policy allows you to define boundaries for security, management, and software distribution based on the structure of your enterprise Active Directory. Windows offers a tool called the Security Configuration Tool Set, which is covered in detail in Chapter 3, and which includes support for managing Group Policy settings destined to be applied to client machines. These settings are grouped into collections, called Group Policy objects (GPOs), that are stored together in a file created with the Group Policy snap-in in the Microsoft Management Console (MMC) application. Microsoft has also just released the Group Policy Management Console, which is a wonderful tool that's quite a bit more intuitive than the administrator applets that ship with Windows 2000 and Windows Server 2003. In this chapter, I'll take a look at configuring enterprise-wide security policies and applying and enforcing them using these Group Policy tools.

System Policies, Group Policies, and Interaction

Policies have, of course, come a long way since the concept was first introduced into a Windows operating system. Windows 95 first contained "System Policy," which was a part of the operating system that was later carried forward into editions of Windows 98, Windows ME, and NT. System Policy hinges on remote administration of a workstation from a central console, hence the inclusion of the Remote Registry Service and Remote Registry Editor application. Its sole purpose was to facilitate making widespread changes to a user's Registry settings—wallpaper, removing system administration applets from the Start menu, and other runtime configurations—without making the administrator visit each workstation.

How did System Policies actually work? It's simpler than you might otherwise believe. Windows would store a copy of the Registry modifications an administrator makes—usually with the Windows Policy Editor, POLEDIT.EXE—in the NETLOGON share on all Windows domain controllers. Microsoft hardcoded instructions into Windows 9x and NT to retrieve a specific file from that share, so there was no real client-side configuration. So a specific user would authenticate to Windows, during the process of which the operating system would retrieve a copy of the appropriate file from the domain controller and apply the user and computer settings in that file to the user's Registry session. The effects of those changes are seen when Windows or an application consults the Registry.

Contrast this setup with Group Policy. Group Policy is made up not of one file sitting on a domain controller share, but of many assorted slices of settings, known as Group Policy objects. These objects, coupled with information on login scripts and the like stored in the SYSVOL shares on any Windows 2000 domain controller, work to create Group Policy as a whole. Whereas with System Policies, only Registry entries could be modified, with Group Policy a whole subset of Windows functions can be controlled. Group Policy provides an interface for controlling Windows's dynamic link libraries—those DLL files that always fill the SYSTEM32 directories on all systems. And also, Microsoft decided that Group Policy would be the only way to manage some subsystems of Windows. You won't find utilities in the Administrative Tools group to manage IP security (IPsec) or other lower-level operating system functions; you'll have to depend on Group Policy for that.

Now those without administrative domains in Windows 2000 (in other words, those without Active Directory) aren't necessarily left out in the cold. A common misconception about Group Policy is that it's only available on Active Directory–enabled networks. That isn't the case. Although the functionality of an Active Directory–less Group Policy is more limited, it can still be used. Without AD, Group Policy becomes a limited local administration tool that controls local users, groups, and computer settings, but not those of several computers. You can, however, create and distribute these policies to other Windows 2000 workstations and servers from a central location, though management isn't as simple.

A nice feature of Group Policy is that it automatically replicates its settings and objects to other domain controllers within the same domain. This mimics the functionality of the NT-esque directory replication service that propagated NTCONFIG.POL, the System Policy file for NT machines, from the primary domain controller down to the backup domain controllers. However, without Group Policy and Active Directory, you need to take advantage of the File Replication Service, which is included with Windows 2000. This replicates anything in a domain controller's SYSVOL directory out to other domain controllers. So take heed that the contents of the NETLOGON share on Windows 2000 domain controllers don't automatically replicate.

Mixing Policies and Operating Systems

The water becomes muddied when you examine the environment in which most corporate networks run. There's usually a mix of machines, some 9x, ME, NT, Windows 2000, and XP machines, and servers running NT, 2000, and Server 2003. How do System Policies and Group Policy interact in a world where certain systems listen to some of the policies but not all? There are a few issues to note, and I'll discuss them in this section:

- First, older systems—those running Windows 9x and NT namely—will not recognize or understand Group Policy. But newer systems will understand older policy types. Windows NT machines can't apply Group Policy, because they weren't built to understand it. But Windows 2000 machines can use System Policies from NT domain controllers, because they know System Policies exist and have the logic built in to ask for them.

- Second, Group Policy is refreshed upon user logon and at various, regular intervals throughout a user's session (for user settings) and throughout the time a computer is connected to the network (for computer settings). This is usually done at a domain controller's behest around every 90 minutes or so for workstations and every 5 minutes for servers. System Policies are only retrieved from the domain controller at user logon. They aren't pushed during the day.

- Third, Windows 9x and NT only looks at System Policies from the domain controller that holds the current user's account. This only applies in situations where a machine's account is in a domain separate from a user's personal account, but it's a bit of reverse logic that I don't understand completely. Most System Policy settings adjust computer configurations, so why not apply policies based on machine domains? It's a nonissue at this point, with Group Policy, but it's still something to be aware of.

- Fourth, to further confuse and annoy administrators, Windows 2000 differs from NT in that it responds to policies from BOTH the user and the machine domain. This works with regular NT 4 domains and Active Directory domains. But Windows only applies the parts of the policy that apply to users from the user's domain; it ignores machine policy that resides on a user's domain. The converse is also true: Windows applies machine policies retrieved from the machine domain, but it ignores user policy from the machine domain. Also, just to be different, Windows 2000 retrieves policies from domain controllers throughout the day (not only just upon user logon), even without Active Directory. This halfway emulates the native functionality of Group Policy.

- Fifth, if a domain offers both System Policies and Group Policy, a client machine will only retrieve and apply domain Group Policy objects. It will completely ignore System Policies. Likewise, if a domain only has available System Policies, the system will apply those. If there are conflicts between requirements set by a System Policy and requirements set by a Group Policy object, then the Group Policy object will always be applied. So Group Policy on a domain always trumps System Policies.

- Finally, domain Group Policy objects always trump local Group Policy objects. There are no exceptions to this, because it would make for a huge security hole, thereby giving local administrators more control over a machine than domain administrators have.

Table 5-1 explains the possible outcomes of mixing policy across different operating systems and domain control environments.

Table 5-1. Effects of Using Different Operating Systems in Different Domain Environments

CLIENT OS	USER DOMAIN TYPE	MACHINE DOMAIN TYPE	RESULTING BEHAVIOR
Windows 9x	AD	N/A	Windows will download and apply settings in CONFIG.POL only.
Windows 9x	NT	N/A	Windows will download and apply settings in CONFIG.POL only.

Table 5-1. Effects of Using Different Operating Systems in Different Domain Environments (Continued)

CLIENT OS	USER DOMAIN TYPE	MACHINE DOMAIN TYPE	RESULTING BEHAVIOR
Windows NT	AD	AD	NT will ignore Group Policy objects and only apply settings it receives when it downloads NTCONFIG.POL from the current user account's home domain controller.
Windows NT	AD	NT	NT will ignore Group Policy objects and only apply settings it receives when it downloads NTCONFIG.POL from the current user account's home domain controller.
Windows NT	NT	AD	NT will ignore Group Policy objects and only apply settings it receives when it downloads NTCONFIG.POL from the current user account's home domain controller.
Windows NT	NT	NT	NT downloads NTCONFIG.POL from the current user account's home domain controller.
Windows 2000/XP	AD	AD	Windows applies Group Policies from both domain controllers (user settings from the user domain and computer settings from the machine domain), which are applied in favor of any local Group Policies that might be in effect.

Table 5-1. Effects of Using Different Operating Systems in Different Domain Environments (Continued)

CLIENT OS	USER DOMAIN TYPE	MACHINE DOMAIN TYPE	RESULTING BEHAVIOR
Windows 2000/XP	AD	NT	Windows applies user settings from the domain Group Policy it receives from the user's Active Directory–enabled domain. Windows also downloads NTCONFIG.POL from the machine domain and applies computer settings from it. Domain Group Policies will always win a conflict over both system and local Group Policies, and local Group Policies always win over System Policies.
Windows 2000/XP	NT	AD	Windows applies the user settings from the NTCONFIG.POL it downloads from the user's home domain. It applies domain Group Policy objects found in Active Directory in the machine's home domain.
Windows 2000/XP	NT	NT	Windows downloads System Policy files from each domain controller and applies the user settings from the user domain's NTCONFIG.POL and the computer settings from the machine domain's NTCONFIG.POL. If local Group Policies are in effect on the workstation itself, they override any System Policies downloaded from domain controllers.

Security and the Group Policy Framework

Windows Group Policy allows you to configure security options that reside inside Group Policy objects that apply to certain partitions and boundaries inside your organization's Active Directory. The Group Policy Framework defines seven areas in which Group Policy can manage security settings across an Active Directory structure. Table 5-2 describes them.

Table 5-2. Group Policy Framework Security Settings

FRAMEWORK AREA	DESCRIPTION
Account area	This framework area applies security configuration to user accounts, including passwords, account lockouts, and Kerberos ticket policies. Password and account-lockout policies apply to workstations and servers; Kerberos ticket policies apply only to domain controllers.
Local policies	This area allows you to set auditing and event-logging policies, user rights assignments, and Registry keys that directly affect system security. Settings in this area apply to all Windows 2000 or later systems, and not only to a specific type.
Restricted groups	This particularly useful group allows you to define policies regarding a user's membership into security groups that allow elevated privileges. It's simple to define a policy where domain users can never be a member of the local Administrators group; other policies are equally easy.
System services	Here you can set startup options for services and access controls on them.
Registry	In this area you can configure access permissions on specific keys in the Registry.
Public key policies	You can establish settings for encrypted recovery agents for the Windows encrypting file system (EFS), certificate authorities for a specific Windows domain, trusted certificate authorities, and other public cryptography options.
IPsec policies on Active Directory	This area allows you to define IPsec configurations for any given unit in your Active Directory.

Organized Layout of Policies

With power comes complexity, and Group Policy is no exception. Many hours of Windows administrators' lives have been squandered on basic troubleshooting of Group Policy. Answers to quandaries such as "Why isn't this policy in effect on this system?" or "I thought I turned OFF IPsec!" can be difficult to track down if your Active Directory is full of GPOs that are applied inconsistently, redundantly, and inappropriately.

To curtail your security policies and make them easier to locate, disable, change, and apply, try to follow the guidelines listed here.

NOTE *Although the focus of this chapter is on the Group Policy Security Framework, the majority of this general advice works for any GPO you wish to deploy.*

- Group your policies logically and define boundaries to contain them. Although your Active Directory may be organized by geographic location, your system management needs might revolve around a different paradigm. For example, you may need IPsec for all company executives' laptops, but they might not all be in your New York office. Or all middle managers in your corporation might require a customized version of Internet Explorer that doesn't lock them out from accessing the Internet, which might be the default configuration for all computers in the domain. The idea is to map out the kinds of restrictions you need, and then define boundaries to which those policies apply. This will make it easier to apply them to the target users and computers even if the geographical and managerial boundaries do not match.

- Inside those boundaries, configure policies that represent common values in your organization. Do you normally configure workstations in your finance department to lock a computer after three unsuccessful logon attempts? Does a particular domain in your forest need additional desktop restrictions—should they not be allowed to run Control Panel? Change their wallpaper? Install software on their own? These are the kinds of policy sets that probably sound familiar. Group these together and create GPOs for each of these like sets of policy settings.

- Configure organizational units inside Active Directory that contain machines grouped according to like roles or functions within an organization. This gets further into the granulation of your security policies. For example, Windows comes by default with domain controllers residing in a separate organizational unit in Active Directory. You might consider putting desktops, laptops, and servers into their own organizational units, which make it easier to apply policies solely to laptops—such as requiring the use of the EFS.

Continuing with that train of thought, I'll now give you an understatement: It can require some work to configure Group Policy correctly and effectively. The most difficult parts of the process are planning and laying out the policy settings; Windows takes care of the actual deployment to client computers, which is one of the features that makes Group Policy a compelling management tool. This ease of deployment is a double-edged sword, however. It's equally simple to misconfigure an access control list or change a setting (anybody who has played with the Require Signed Communications settings know this all too well) and wreak utter havoc on your domain.

Even more difficult sometimes is getting the big picture. That is to say, it's hard to see how your Active Directory layout and structure—which probably mimics your organization's hierarchical personnel structure logically and traditionally—can coexist with Group Policy objects, which seem to cross hierarchy boundaries and rely on other scopes of an application. With careful planning however, Group Policy can overlay your existing directory structure and complement it with its own management boundaries.

Policy Application Precedence

It's important to note that security policies applied on certain levels take precedence over others. Active Directory–applied policies (those that are applied to organizational units and domains) take precedence over any locally set policy. If you're familiar with Group Policy, you'll recall that this order is very similar to any policy set with Group Policy. This precedence order, when active, can result in system configurations that are vastly different than those associated with Windows NT systems.

Figure 5-1 describes the order and precedence with which Group Policy objects are applied.

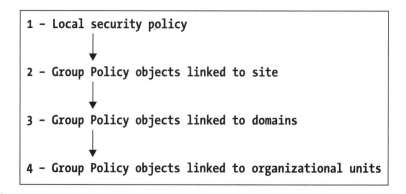

1 - Local security policy

2 - Group Policy objects linked to site

3 - Group Policy objects linked to domains

4 - Group Policy objects linked to organizational units

Figure 5-1. Windows's application of Group Policy objects on a given system

Creating Security Configuration Files

The easiest way to create the necessary security configuration files is to use the Security Configuration Tool Set, which contains snap-ins to the pervasive Microsoft Management Console management application. The relevant snap-ins are as follows:

- **Security Settings Extension to Group Policy:** Provides a direct path to security configuration for domains and organizational units.

- **Active Directory Users and Computers:** Is the usual tool to administer the directory store, its contents, and various settings and permissions on the objects therein.

- **Security Templates:** Provides the GUI to create the security configuration files. This was covered in Chapter 3.

The Security Settings Extension to Group Policy can only configure computer policy, not user policy, as opposed to generic Group Policy, which can apply to both. However, certain security policies, mainly dealing with public keys, certificates, and cryptography, can be managed on a user basis and not just by machine. Consult a general Group Policy reference for more information on this.

Loading the Group Policy Snap-in

To get started, you'll need to load the Group Policy snap-in to the MMC. Use the following procedure to do so:

1. Use a command line to execute the command **mmc /s.**

2. Select Add/Remove Snap-in from the Console menu. In the dialog box that is raised, click the Add button.

3. The Available Standalone Snap-in list appears. Click Group Policy, and then click the Add button.

4. Click Browse in the Select Group Policy Object dialog box (see Figure 5-2).

5. In the Browse for a Group Policy Object dialog box, add the various GPOs that you wish to manage, and click OK.

6. Click Finish, and then OK, to conclude the procedure.

If your machine isn't a member of the domain, you can still use Group Policy, but its functionality will be a bit more limited. The only exposed settings to a nondomained machine are located within the Local Security Policy Console, which can be found inside the Administrative Tools folder in the Control Panel.

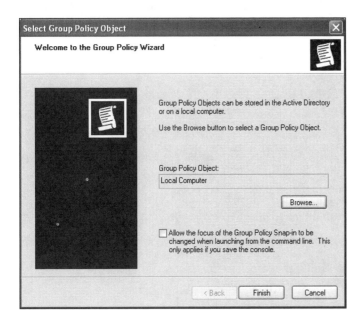

Figure 5.2: The Select Group Policy Object dialog box

Default Domain Policy

When you install Windows 2000 or later, a default domain security policy is created. It's a simple task to use this default policy as a base and add and customize settings based on your individual implementation. Let's take a look at this default policy first, and then work through customizing it.

To view the default domain security policy, do the following:

1. Open the Active Directory Users and Computers snap-in.

2. Expand the domain tree corresponding to your domain's name in the left pane.

3. Right-click the domain name and select Properties.

4. Click the Group Policy tab, select Default Domain Policy in the details box, and then click the Edit button. Windows raises the Group Policy window.

5. To view each of the default domain policies, drill down through Computer Configuration ➢ Windows Settings ➢ Security Settings, and click Account Policies.

6. Look at the right pane. You should see Password Policy, Account Lockout Policy, and Kerberos Policy, and by clicking on each you can view or change the default configuration of them.

Default Domain Controller Security Policies

You'll need to use the Group Policy MMC snap-in to look at the default security policy on the domain controller organizational unit. Do the following to access the snap-in:

1. Load the snap-in as described earlier in the chapter. Ensure that you selected the Domain Controllers.yourdomain.com object in step 4 of the previous list.

2. In the left pane, drill down through Computer Configuration ➢ Windows Settings ➢ Security Settings.

3. Click Account Policies. In the right pane, you should see the possible security options for this organizational unit.

The special way that account policies are distributed to domain controllers deserves comment. All domain controllers in a specific domain will apply security policies established at the domain level no matter where the actual computer object for that domain controller resides in Active Directory. This helps to ensure that consistent account policies apply to any domain accounts. All other policies are applied at the normal hierarchical level, both to domain controllers and to other workstations and servers in the domain. Only domain controllers are affected by this special exception. Just a tip to remember when you're planning account policy distribution among your organizational units.

You can view a domain controller's effective security policy by doing the following:

1. Choose Start, click Run, and type **GPEdit.msc.** The Group Policy Editor will open.

2. In the left pane, drill down through Computer Configuration ➢ Windows Settings ➢ Security Settings, and click Local Policies.

You can now view the domain controller's effective security policy. When you're finished, close the Group Policy\Local Computer Policy snap-in. When prompted to save console settings, click No, unless you've done something you'd like to hold on to.

At this point, you now have all the tools to begin pushing automated security configurations to clients running Windows 2000 and later. All of the settings covered so far in this book, unless noted at the time, are fair game for distribution under Group Policy. Now, I'll focus for a bit on how to fix problems when Group Policy goes awry.

Troubleshooting Group Policy

The process of diagnosing what's going on with Group Policy and why it isn't doing what you want it to do can be infuriating at times. Use the steps recommended in the following section to assist you in tracking down where your problem lies.

DNS problems can plague your network and make it nearly impossible for Group Policy objects to be applied. This problem mainly manifests itself in the requirements for logging on to a domain. Without DNS, you still might be able to authenticate to a domain controller, but Group Policy objects will simply break. That's because they require various types of DNS subrecords, known as SRV records, so that you can know which computer has which service to manage. This is a good place to start looking if Group Policy simply doesn't function.

If you're a seasoned network professional, you'll be familiar with the concept of inheritance. This can also be a stumbling block with Group Policy. Beware of a couple of options. One, the No Override function, which does nothing more than cease the processing of any Group Policy objects under the object on which the option is set. Conversely, also be wary of the Block Inheritance function, which stops the processing of GPOs that reside above the object on which the object is set. This is a case of knowing what you set and properly documenting it, but it can still eat up hours upon hours of troubleshooting time.

Another issue you might see is that of Group Policy distribution and synchronization. Distribution and synchronization both rely on a versioning system managed internally by Windows that keeps track of unique revisions of the two parts of a Group Policy object. These are the Group Policy container, which is associated with a particular organizational structure in Active Directory, and the Group Policy template, which is a file located in the SYSVOL\Policies directory. These are normally pushed out from the Windows 2000 or Windows Server 2003 domain controller that's in the PDC emulator role and sent to all the other domain controllers in a given domain. But if the versioning system is wrong or somehow corrupted, this distribution may not completely finish, or it might not even occur at all. Windows comes with a couple of tools that will help you fish out the nonstandard Group Policy objects: GPOTOOL, REPLMON, and the newly available Group Policy Management Console (see the Microsoft website for more) can all help you see these objects. Look at logs on the affected domain controllers and see if any errors can help you determine the cause.

Along the same lines is actually realizing when Group Policy objects are distributed, retrieved, and applied. Earlier in the chapter I pointed out that the interval Windows 2000 uses to push out new Group Policy objects is 90 minutes for workstations and regular member servers and 5 minutes for domain controllers. But this is only for new or revised Group Policy objects. If there have been no Group Policy changes, nothing is pushed unless you manually do so, either from the command line or through another systemwide policy that pushes policy regardless of whether a change has occurred. So remember that local configuration changes won't necessarily be corrected by Group Policy unless either the domain Group Policy object itself changes or you force a refresh of Group Policy.

Checkpoints

If you're in a hurry, the highlights of this chapter include the following:

- Group your policies logically and define boundaries to contain them.

- Inside those boundaries, configure policies that represent common values in your organization.

- Configure organizational units inside Active Directory that contain machines grouped according to like roles, or functions within an organization.

- Adjust the default domain security policy to encompass a common security configuration to be deployed across all systems in your domain.

- Adjust the default domain controller security policy to more secure settings that should be applied to all machines serving that role in your Active Directory.

- Use the Computer Configuration nodes in Group Policy to adjust machine-specific settings regardless of the logged-on user.

- Use the User Configuration nodes in Group Policy to adjust user-specific settings that will follow the person across all machines in the policy's scope.

And if you're having Group Policy problems, here's a rundown of things to look for:

- Check your domain's DNS configuration to make sure SRV subrecords are being properly registered.

- Make sure that the No Override and Block Inheritance functionality of Group Policy isn't hindering the application of Group Policy objects.

- Examine your domain controller logs to see if the File Replication Service is throwing any errors related to the versioning of GPT files.

- Force a refresh of Group Policy from a domain controller's command line if all else fails.

CHAPTER 6

Patch Management

THE BANE OF EVERY ADMINISTRATOR'S EXISTENCE. The pain in the rear of system management. That never-ceasing headache that pounds at CIOs everywhere. You might have guessed by now that I'm speaking of patch management.

And I use the term "management" loosely. As I write this there are more than 40 updates that need to be applied to a new Dell computer running Windows XP. There were over 20 updates for Windows 2000 Service Pack 3 that needed to be applied to new systems before Microsoft released Service Pack 4 in the summer of 2003. This ever-growing hairball of security fixes, bug fixes, critical updates, and patch revisions has almost gotten to the point where it would be easier to disconnect all machines from the Internet and work with stone tablets than deploy new systems.

It shouldn't be that way, and Microsoft realizes that. They've come out with a tool that's not perfect, that has limited functionality, and isn't very flexible. But it's got two great things going for it: It's timely, and it works fairly well. That product is Software Update Services (SUS), and this chapter will focus on installing, implementing, and administering SUS on your network. I'll also cover a comparison between SUS and a flagship network and system-management product (Systems Management Server), and how to monitor SUS for failures.

About Software Update Services

As part of its Strategic Technology Protection Program, Microsoft sought to use its Windows Update technology—the software that runs the universal update site for all but the oldest versions of Windows. SUS at this point does NOT focus on adding new features to already released software; it's only concerned with critical updates that allow administrators to somewhat easily deploy critical updates to servers running Windows 2000 or Windows Server 2003, and desktop computers running Windows 2000 Professional or Windows XP Professional. It's designed to work especially in networks with an Active Directory implementation, but it will function without one.

Installing SUS on your network requires the following two elements:

- One server connected to the Internet running the actual server component of SUS. This machine acts as a local version of the public Windows Update site, which contains critical updates and service packs for all supported operating systems. This server synchronizes with the public Windows Update site on a schedule that the corporate administrator selects. That administrator then approves or rejects the availability of certain updates on the SUS server. You can also have multiple SUS servers on an intranet and configure which client machines are directed to specific SUS servers for updates.

- The Automatic Updates feature of Windows 2000 Service Pack 3 and higher or Windows XP Professional at any revision level. Directed by a Registry change or an applied Group Policy object, the client computers that are running this Automatic Updates feature are sent to the local network's SUS server on a set schedule to download updates appropriate to their machines. The SUS server will analyze the operating system, service-pack level, and any currently installed updates, and push only those updates that are both needed AND approved by the administrator beforehand.

Comparing Software Update Services to Systems Management Server

Microsoft's SUS, as mentioned before, is only concerned with deploying critical updates to modern, post-2000 NT-based operating systems. The flagship administrative product from Redmond, called Systems Management Server (SMS), is quite a bit more flexible than SUS, but it also costs thousands of dollars more. For the price tag (which was free at press time), however, SUS offers a decent value. What does SMS offer that SUS doesn't have? Table 6-1 lists the update features of both management solutions, and compares and contrasts them.

Table 6-1. Stackup of SUS against SMS

ASPECT	SOFTWARE UPDATE SERVICES	SMS WITH SUS PACK
Content	SUS will automatically download critical updates on a schedule from the public Windows Update site.	SMS will automatically download updates as well, but not just critical updates. Features, bug fixes, and security updates are available to be deployed through SMS.

Table 6-1. Stackup of SUS against SMS (Continued)

ASPECT	SOFTWARE UPDATE SERVICES	SMS WITH SUS PACK
Geographical Distribution	Multiple SUS servers on a local network will synchronize updates from other servers on the network or from a central network share.	SMS is designed to distribute packages and software across both LAN and WAN links, including updates on a schedule and sensitivity to overall bandwidth cost and speed.
Installation	Schedules can be set through Group Policy or through a Registry key entry. The downloading of updates takes advantage of background inactivity and includes fault-tolerant features.	The scheduling with SMS is very flexible and can be based on any number of factors. You can also target updates to certain groups, organizational units, network subnets, and inventory groups.
Status	SUS uses Internet Information Services' built-in logs for reporting functionality.	SMS has native reporting functionality, including the ability to filter data on multiple levels.
Targeting	A machine that connects to its assigned SUS server downloads all relevant patches that have been approved by an administrator.	Updates can be targeted to certain groups, organization units, network subnets, and inventory groups.

According to Microsoft, SMS will be receiving security patch management updates in the third quarter of 2003. These updates consist of a feature pack addition and various enhancements to the distribution selection methods within the product. On top of that, the newest version, SMS 2003, will include this functionality built in, without the need for a service or feature pack.

If you already have a patch management solution in place, stick with that. There's likely nothing in SUS that would entice you to change your existing solution, at least with regards to the current revision. Particularly, if you're using SMS to distribute patches, you should use the latest feature-pack release when it becomes generally available. SUS is meant to be a free, reduced-functionality alternative that gets the bare minimum done. Although it's ideal for small and medium-sized organizations, larger businesses will probably find the money spent on implementing SMS less than the man-hours spent deploying SUS and working around its limitations.

Using Software Update Services: On the Server Side

There are a few phases to the SUS installation. First, you should download and install the software:

1. Go to the SUS website at http://www.microsoft.com/sus.

2. Download Sus10sp1.exe to a folder on the server where you want to either install SUS 1.0 SP1 or apply the service pack to an existing installation of SUS 1.0.

3. Double-click the file using the server on which you want to install or upgrade SUS.

4. Click Next on the Welcome screen to continue.

5. Decide whether to accept or reject the license agreement, and click Next.

6. Select the Typical checkbox unless there's a good reason for you to use a custom installation. Click Next.

7. Make a note of the location with which you can direct clients to SUS. Click Install to begin the actual file copy.

8. When the file copy is finished, make a note of the location of the SUS administrative pages. Then click Finish to exit the wizard.

The administrative website for SUS will open. The default address for these pages is http://SUSServerName/SUSAdmin. You can also navigate through Start ➤ Programs ➤ Administrative Tools, and click Microsoft Software Update Services. You'll see something much like that in Figure 6-1.

The first step is to configure the options for your SUS server. In the left pane, click Set Options. The sections on this page are described here:

- **Select a proxy server configuration:** This option tells SUS whether to connect to the Windows Update website using a proxy server or to simply use a direct Internet connection. Fill out this form in much the same way that you would Internet Explorer's options.

- **Specify the name your clients use to locate this update server:** Here you configure how the server will respond to update requests from client computers on your network. I recommend using the full DNS name here and not just a NetBIOS name for maximum compatibility and performance.

- **Select which server to synchronize content from:** Here you can instruct SUS to download updates to distribute to client computers directly from the public Windows Update site. In addition, you can elect to download from another SUS server located somewhere on your network, or from a manually created network share. You can also select whether to use the list of approved updates from other SUS servers or to use only that server's store in tandem with the local server's list of approved updates.

- **Select how you want to handle new versions of previously applied updates:** If a new version of a patch or other hotfix is issued, you can select here whether to automatically approve the revision for distribution or to treat it as a new patch that needs to be manually approved by an administrator.

- **Select where you want to store updates:** You can select whether to download the updates from Windows Update in real time or batch-download them and store them on the SUS server. You can also select the localities for which you'd like to store critical updates and security hotfixes (although I've found that this filter doesn't always work as expected).

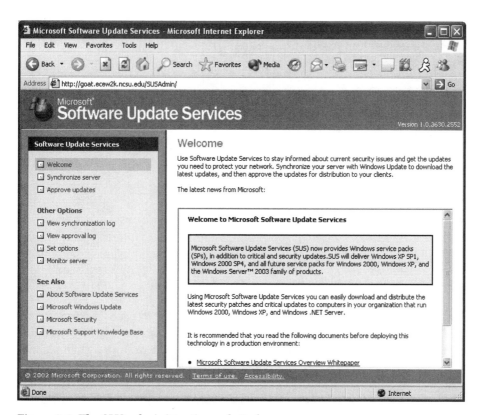

Figure 6-1. The SUS administrative website home page

Synchronizing and Approving Content

When you start the content synchronization process, the SUS server goes out to either the public Windows Update servers or another local SUS server (as configured in the "Set Options" section) and downloads the entire library of available critical updates and service packs for each language you've configured. This synchronization usually results in about 150 MB worth of data being transferred for just English updates, or close to 600 MB of data for updates in every localization.

To synchronize content, surf to the SUS administrative website, and then do the following:

1. In the left-hand Navigation pane, click Synchronize Server.

2. Click the Synchronize Now button in the right pane to begin the transfer.

You can also opt to schedule your synchronizations automatically, so that you don't have to remember to resynchronize every time a new update is released—which is all too often in my opinion. On the Synchronize Server page, click Synchronization Schedule. A dialog box like the one in Figure 6-2 will appear.

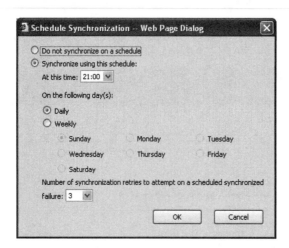

Figure 6-2. Setting a synchronization schedule for the SUS host machine

Set your desired options for synchronization and then click OK. Be aware that if the SUS server can't connect to the appropriate upstream update source, it will repeat its attempts four times, and space out each attempt by half an hour. You can adjust this using the Number of Synchronization Retries to Attempt on a

Scheduled Synchronization Failure drop-down list in the Schedule
Synchronization dialog box shown previously.

Now that you have an actual library of updates on or near your SUS host
machine, you can approve the updates individually for distribution to client
machines within your network. The approval process makes it easy to withhold
patches until further testing is done, which partly assuages the general fear that's
caused by installing patches that might cause more problems than they fix.
To begin the update approval process, do the following:

1. In the Navigation pane, click Approve Updates.

2. In the right-hand pane, select the updates that you would like to
   approve, and click Approve when you've finished your selection.

SUS will notify you when the approval is complete. In the right-hand pane,
where all the updates are shown, each patch's status is shown as one of five possible values. A new update is one that was just recently downloaded and hasn't
been approved yet. An approved update is available for distribution to each
client machine. An update that isn't approved will not be distributed to clients,
but the actual patch file remains in the library on the SUS host machine. An
updated patch indicates a new version of an earlier patch that currently exists in
the library. And finally, a temporarily unavailable patch is one whose dependent
files were downloaded incorrectly, could not be found, or were otherwise unable
to be located by SUS.

If, for some reason, you would like to clear the list of approved updates,
you can clear all checkboxes on the list of available updates and then click
Approve. This will remove any available updates from the SUS catalog, and your
client machines will stop downloading the updates until you approve more fixes.
This will not, however, uninstall the patches from the client machines.

The SUS server will record an entry to the synchronization log whenever the
server attempts to connect to its upstream provider. You can access this log from
the SUS administrative website using any standard web browser; you can also
access it directly from the SUS host machine in the autoupdate\administration
directory of the SUS website (the file name is history-Sync.xml). The log entry
contains the time of the last sync, whether the operation was completed, the
date and time of the next-scheduled synchronization, the contents of the operation, whether each component was successfully installed, and whether the
synchronization was routine or manual.

The SUS server also keeps a log of all approved updates, which you
can find in the same place as the synchronization log with the file name
history-approve.xml.

Pushing Out the Automated Updates Client

If you're upgrading an installation of SUS 1.0, the Automatic Update software installed on your client computers will self-update to the latest SUS 1.0 SP1 client software. This will occur after the SUS 1.0 server has been successfully updated to SP1 and synchronized with the latest content available on the Windows Update servers.

You can install the updated Automatic Updates client on your clients by using the MSI install package, self-updating from the old Critical Update Notification (CUN) tool, installing Windows 2000 Service Pack 3 or 4, installing Windows XP Service Pack 1, or installing Windows Server 2003.

You can download the Automatic Updates client from the Microsoft website at the SUS web page, located at `http://www.microsoft.com/sus`. On a standalone machine, the AU client can simply be added by running the WUAU22.MSI file on the machine.

Manually installing a file can quickly become a pain when you have more than just a few machines to handle. Fortunately, because the client installation program is in the form of an MSI, you can easily push the program to clients by using Group Policy. To create a new GPO, assign it to your computers, and then have it installed automatically.

 NOTE *The application will be installed in the context of the local computer, so make sure that authenticated users have rights on the source folders.*

1. Open the Active Directory Users and Computers MMC snap-in.

2. Right-click the domain or organizational unit to which you're interested in deploying the client, and select Properties.

3. Click the Group Policy tab.

4. Click New to create a new Group Policy object (GPO). Type in a name for the GPO.

5. Select the new GPO from the list, and click Edit to open the Group Policy Object Editor.

6.   Expand Computer Configuration, and then select Software Settings.

7.   Right-click Software Installation in the left pane, select New, and then click Package.

8.   Enter the path to WUAU22.msi. Make sure you use a network path and not a local path to ensure that your clients can find the file at boot time. Click Open.

9.   Choose Assigned to assign the package to the computers in the domain or organizational unit, and then click OK.

10. Allow time for polices to replicate through the domain. Usually this is accomplished within 15 minutes.

11. Restart the client computers. The client software should be installed before the Logon dialog box is displayed.

You can also deploy the client MSI through a logon script by calling MSIEXEC followed by the client software file name as an argument. The software will be installed as requested.

Configuring the Automatic Updates Client

The Automatic Updates client doesn't have any user-interface options for determining the origin of updates to install. You must set this with either a Registry change on each of the client computers or through Group Policy, either locally or based through a domain.

Through a domain-based Group Policy, direct clients to the SUS server should use the following procedure:

1.   Open the Default Domain Policy GPO in Active Directory Users and Computers and click the Edit button.

2.   Expand Computer Configuration, Administrative Templates, and Windows Components.

3.   Select Windows Update. The right pane will contain four options that pertain to the Automatic Updates client, as depicted in Figure 6-3.

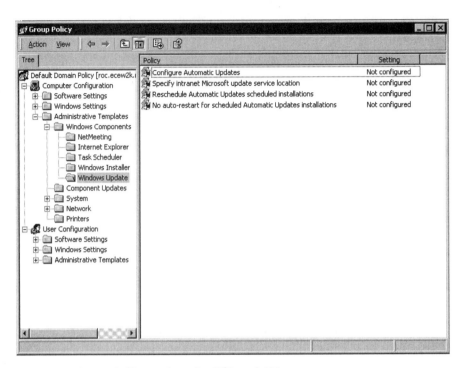

Figure 6-3. Group Policy options for SUS and AU

These options are described here in more detail:

- **Configure Automatic Updates:** This option specifies whether this computer will receive security updates and critical bug fixes. The first option
makes sure that the currently logged-on user is notified before downloading updates. The user will then be notified again before installing the
downloaded updates. The second option ensures that updates will automatically be downloaded, but not installed until a logged-on user
acknowledges the updates' presence and authorizes the installation. The
third option makes sure that updates are automatically downloaded and
installed on a schedule that you can set in the appropriate boxes on the
sheet. To use this setting, click Enabled, and then select one of the options.

- **Specify Intranet Microsoft Update Service Location:** This option designates an SUS server from which to download updates. To use this setting,
you must set two server name values: the server from which the Automatic
Updates client detects and downloads updates, and the server to which
updated workstations upload statistics. You can set both values to be the
same server.

- **Reschedule Automatic Updates Scheduled Installations:** This option specifies the amount of time to wait after booting before continuing with a scheduled installation that was missed previously for whatever reason (power outage, system powered off, network connection lost, and so on). If the status is set to Enabled, a missed scheduled installation will occur the specified number of minutes after the computer is next started. If the status is set to Disabled or Not Configured, a missed scheduled installation will simply roll over to the next scheduled installation.

- **No Auto-restart for Scheduled Automatic Updates Installations:** This option designates whether a client computer should automatically reboot or not when an update that's just installed requires a system restart. If the status is set to Enabled, Automatic Updates will not restart a computer automatically during a scheduled installation if a user is logged in to the computer. Instead, it will notify the user to restart the computer to complete the installation. If the status is set to Disabled or Not Configured, Automatic Updates will notify the user that the computer will automatically restart in 5 minutes to complete the installation.

You will want to allow 10 to 15 minutes for the changes to the domain's policy to replicate among all domain controllers.

To adjust the Group Policy on a machine that isn't managed by Active Directory, follow these steps:

1. Click Start, select Run, and type **GPEDIT.msc** to load the Group Policy snap-in.

2. Expand Computer Configuration and Administrative Templates.

3. Click Add/Remove Templates, and then click Add.

4. Enter the name of the Automatic Updates ADM file, which you can find in the INF subdirectory within your Windows root. In addition, you can find it in the INF subdirectory within the SUS server machine's Windows root.

5. Click Open, and then click Close to load the wuau.adm file.

You can now adjust the policy settings as described in the previous subsection.

Finally, to adjust some of these behavior settings through Registry changes, use the appropriate key for each of the following settings:

- **To enable or disable Automatic Updates:** Create the value NoAutoUpdate in the HKEY_LOCAL_MACHINE\SOFTWARE\Policies\Microsoft\ Windows\WindowsUpdate\AU key. The value is a DWORD with possible values zero (enabled) or one (disabled).

- **To configure the update download and notification behavior:** Create the value AUOptions in the HKEY_LOCAL_MACHINE\SOFTWARE\Policies\ Microsoft\Windows\WindowsUpdate\AU key. The value is a DWORD that includes integers 2 (notify of download and notify before installation), 3 (automatically download but notify before installation), and 4 (automatically download and schedule the installation).

- **To schedule an automated installation:** Create the values ScheduledInstallDay and ScheduledInstallTime in the HKEY_LOCAL_ MACHINE\SOFTWARE\Policies\Microsoft\Windows\WindowsUpdate\AU key. The value for each is a DWORD. For ScheduledInstallDay, the range is from 0 to 7, with 0 indicating every day and 1 through 7 indicating the days of the week, Sunday through Saturday. For ScheduledInstallTime, the range is from 0 to 23, signifying the hour of the day in military time.

- **To specify a particular SUS server to use with the Automatic Updates client:** Create the value UseWUServer in HKEY_LOCAL_MACHINE\ SOFTWARE\Policies\Microsoft\Windows\WindowsUpdate\AU key. The value is a DWORD; set it to 1 to enable the custom SUS server name. Then, create the values WUServer and WUStatusServer in the same key, of types Reg_SZ, and specify the name (with the http://) as the value.

- **To specify how long to wait before completing a missed installation:** Create the value RescheduleWaitTime in the HKEY_LOCAL_MACHINE\ SOFTWARE\Policies\Microsoft\Windows\WindowsUpdate\AU key. The value is a DWORD that ranges from 1 to 60, measured in minutes.

- **To specify whether to restart a scheduled installation with a currently logged-in nonadministrative user:** Create the NoAutoRebootWithLoggedOnUsers value in the HKEY_LOCAL_ MACHINE\SOFTWARE\Policies\Microsoft\Windows\WindowsUpdate\AU key. The value is a DWORD that can be 0, which indicates that a reboot will indeed take place, or 1, which indicates the reboot will be postponed while a user is logged on.

Using SUS: On the Client Side

To configure Windows XP to work with SUS, first enable the Automatic Updates feature. In Windows XP, do the following:

1. Open the Control Panel. Navigate to the System applet and open it.

2. Click the Automatic Updates tab.

In Windows 2000, do the following:

1. Open the Control Panel.

2. Navigate to the Automatic Updates applet and double-click it to open it.

You'll see the System Properties dialog box for the feature, as shown in Figure 6-4.

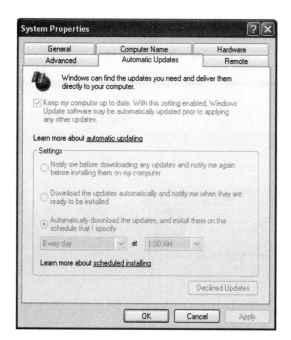

Figure 6-4. Automatic Updates in Windows XP and Windows 2000

As the administrator, you select how updates are downloaded, signaled to the user, and subsequently installed on client machines. The currently logged-on user, if that person happens to have administrator credentials, is notified through a small update icon in the system tray as well as an information "bubble" that pops up when the updates' download is complete. In addition, an administrator can determine if updates have been downloaded by looking at the system log. If the current user isn't an administrator, Windows will wait until one logs on to offer the notification that updates are available for installation.

Update Download and Installation

The updates are downloaded in the session's background by the Background Intelligent Transfer Service (BITS), which is an extension to Windows. BITS detects inactivity over a network connection and uses it to download large amounts of data from remote sites. BITS will detect when a user initiates activity over a connection and pause the download process, waiting for the next idle period to resume it.

On the Automatic Updates property sheet, click the first option to have the currently logged-on user notified before downloading updates. The user will then be notified again before installing the downloaded updates. Use the second option if you want updates automatically downloaded, but want to wait until a logged-on user acknowledges their presence and authorizes the installation. Finally, click the third option if you want updates automatically downloaded and installed on a schedule that you can set in the boxes.

The update installation process proceeds depending on what you select in the boxes. When updates have finished downloading, the notification bubble will appear in the system-tray area of the machine, and an administrative user can double-click the bubble to open the Ready to Install dialog box, shown in Figure 6-5.

Figure 6-5. Automatic Updates dialog box for installation

You can click the Remind Me Later button to defer the installation of updates for a set period of time, ranging from half an hour to three days from the current time.

If you've configured Automatic Updates to install fixes on a regular schedule, the updates will be downloaded in the background and automatically installed on that schedule. Automatic Updates installs the update and restarts the computer if an update requires that, even if there's no local administrator logged on. If an administrator is logged on, she will have the chance to cancel the process; if a normal user is logged on, he will receive a notification of the impending process and a countdown to its initiation. However, between the set install time and the current time, if updates have finished downloading the notification will appear in the system tray as described earlier in this section. The user will not have the option to click Remind Me Later, but he can choose to install the updates at that time to have the process over with before the predetermined installation time.

Monitoring the Client-Side System

SUS and the Automatic Updates client provide several event templates that are written to the system event log to describe the current status of the update process, any errors that are encountered, and a brief notation of what updates were successfully installed. You can program an event-log monitoring tool to monitor for certain event IDs that are specific to SUS. This tool will give you a picture of your network's health with regards to updates. Table 6-2 lists these events and their meanings and contexts.

Table 6-2. SUS and AU Client Event Log Messages

EVENT ID	LABEL	DESCRIPTION
16	Unable to connect	The client can't connect to either the Windows Update site or the SUS server, but will continue trying indefinitely.
17	Install ready; no recurring schedule	Updates have been downloaded and are ready to be installed, but an administrator must log on and manually start the installation process.
18	Install ready; recurring schedule	Updates have been downloaded and are ready to be installed. The date this install is scheduled to occur is listed within the event description.
19	Install success	Updates have been successfully installed; these have been listed.

Table 6-2. SUS and AU Client Event Log Messages (Continued)

EVENT ID	LABEL	DESCRIPTION
20	Install failure	Some updates didn't install correctly; these have been listed.
21	Restart required; no recurring schedule	Updates have been installed, but a reboot is required, and until this reboot is complete Windows cannot fetch more updates for installation. Any user can reboot the machine.
22	Restart required; recurring schedule	Updates have been installed, but a reboot is required and has been scheduled within five minutes.

Checkpoints

If you take nothing else from this chapter, soak in these key points and strategies:

- Don't do anything else until you have some sort of patch-management system installed and running on your network. It WILL BE a priority one of these days if your network is connected to the Internet.

- Deploy SUS unless you have a large business that would benefit from SMS, unless you're already running SMS, or unless you've already got a sufficient patch-management system in place.

- Set SUS to automatically synchronize on a daily basis, so that you receive updates as soon as possible after they're released.

- Approve only the updates for localizations that you maintain. There's no need to have the Japanese version of a patch if you have no Japanese-installed Windows machines.

- Use Group Policy or some other automated method to deploy the Automated Updates client to machines that aren't currently running at least Windows 2000 Service Pack 3 or Windows XP Service Pack 1.

- Enable Automatic Updates on your network.

- Schedule update installations at least weekly, if not daily.

- Educate your users about the ramifications of not keeping their systems updated.

- Use event-log monitoring software to ensure that SUS continues to function correctly.

- Did I mention not to do anything else until you have some sort of patch-management system installed and working on your network?

CHAPTER 7

Network Access
Quarantine Control

ONE OF THE EASIEST AND ARGUABLY most prevalent ways for nefarious software or Internet users to creep onto your network is not through holes in your firewall, or brute-force password attacks, or anything else that might occur at your corporate headquarters or campus. It's through your mobile users, when they try to connect to your business network while on the road.

Let's consider why that is the case. Most remote users are only authenticated on the basis of their identity; no effort is made to verify that their hardware and software meets a certain baseline requirement. Remote users could—and do every day—fail any or all of the following:

- The latest service pack and the latest security hotfixes are installed.

- The corporation-standard antivirus software is installed and running, and the latest signature files are being used.

- Internet or network routing is disabled.

- Windows XP's Internet Connection Firewall (ICF), or any other approved firewall, is installed, enabled, and actively protecting ports on the computer.

You would expect your business desktops to follow policy, but in the past, mobile users have traditionally been forgotten or grudgingly accepted as exceptions to the rule. However, Windows Server 2003 includes a new feature in its Resource Kit, called Network Access Quarantine Control (NAQC), which allows you to prevent remote users from connecting to your network with machines that aren't up to date and secure. This chapter will detail how this feature works and how to install and configure it.

How Network Access Quarantine Works

NAQC prevents unhindered, free access to a network from a remote location until after the destination computer has verified that the remote computer's configuration meets certain requirements and standards as outlined in a script.

To use NAQC, your remote-access computers must be running any of the following: Windows 98 Second Edition, Windows Millennium Edition, Windows 2000, or Windows XP Home or Professional. These versions of Windows support a connectoid that contains the connection information, the baseline script, and a notifier component, which you can create using the Connection Manager Administration Kit (CMAK) in Server 2003. Additionally, you'll need at least one back-end Windows Server 2003 machine that's running an approved listening component; for the purpose of this chapter, I'll assume you're running the Remote Access Quarantine Agent service (called RQS.EXE) from the Windows Server 2003 Resource Kit. Finally, you'll need an NAQC-compliant RADIUS server, such as the Internet Authentication Service in Server 2003, so that you can restrict network access.

Under NAQC, when a connection is established, the destination computers give the remote, connecting computer an IP address, but a "quarantine mode" is established.

In quarantine mode, the following restrictions are in effect:

- A set of packet filters is enabled that restricts the traffic sent to and received from a remote-access client.

- A session timer is enabled that limits the duration of a remote client's connection in quarantine mode before being terminated.

Once the remote computer is in quarantine mode, the baseline script is run. If Windows runs the script and is satisfied with the result, it contacts the listening service running on the Server 2003 back-end machine and reports this result. Quarantine mode is then removed and normal network access is restored. Otherwise, the client is eventually disconnected when the session timer reaches the configured limit as described previously.

A Step-by-Step Overview of Network Access Quarantine Control

Here is a detailed outline of how the connection and quarantining process works, assuming you're using RQC.EXE on the client end from the CMAK and RQS.EXE on the back end from the Resource Kit.

1. The remote user connects his computer, using the quarantined Connection Manager (CM) profile, to the quarantine-enabled connection point, which is usually a machine running the Routing and Remote Access Service (RRAS).

2. The remote user authenticates.

3. RRAS sends a RADIUS Access-Request message to the RADIUS server—in this case, a Server 2003 machine running the Internet Authentication Service (IAS).

4. The IAS server verifies the remote user's credentials successfully and checks its remote-access policies. The connection attempt matches the configured quarantine policy.

5. The connection is accepted, but with quarantine restrictions in place. The IAS server sends a RADIUS Access-Accept message, including the MS-Quarantine-IPFilter and MS-Quarantine-Session-Timeout attributes, to RRAS.

6. The remote user completes the remote-access connection with the RRAS server, which includes leasing an IP address and establishing other network settings.

7. RRAS configures the MS-Quarantine-IPFilter and MS-Quarantine-Session-Timeout settings for the connection, now in quarantine mode. At this point, the remote user can only send traffic that matches the quarantine filters—all other traffic is filtered. It can only remain connected for the value, in seconds, of the MS-Quarantine-Session-Timeout attribute before the quarantine baseline script must be run and the result reported back to RRAS.

8. The CMAK profile runs the quarantine script, currently defined as the "postconnect action."

9. The quarantine script runs and verifies that the remote-access client computer's configuration meets a baseline. If so, the script runs RQC.EXE with its command-line parameters, including a text string representing the version of the quarantine script being used.

10. RQC.EXE sends a notification to RRAS, indicating that the script ended successfully.

11. The notification is received by RQS.EXE on the back end.

12. The listener component on the RRAS server verifies the script version string in the notification message with those configured in the Registry of the RRAS, and returns a message indicating that the script version was either valid or invalid.

13. If the script version was acceptable, RQS.EXE calls the MprAdminConnectionRemoveQuarantine() API, which indicates to RRAS that it's time to remove the MS-Quarantine-IPFilter and MS-Quarantine-Session-Timeout settings from the connection and reconfigure the session for normal network access.

14. Once this is done, the remote user has normal access to the resources on the network.

15. RQS.EXE creates an event describing the quarantined connection in the system event log.

Deploying NAQC

In this section, you'll look at the actual deployment of NAQC on your network. There are six steps, each outlined in separate subsections ahead.

Creating Quarantined Resources

The first step is to create resources that you can actually access while the quarantine packet filters are in place for a remote client. Examples of such resources include DNS servers and DHCP servers, so you can retrieve IP address and connection information and file servers that will download the appropriate software to update out-of-compliance machines. In addition, you can retrieve web servers that may describe the quarantining process or allow a remote user to contact IT support via email if any problems occur.

There are two ways you can specify and use a quarantined resource. The first is to identify certain servers on your network because these quarantine resources without regard to their physical or network location. This allows you to use existing machines to host the quarantined resources, but you also have to create individual packet filters for quarantined sessions for each of these existing machines. For performance and overhead reasons, it's best to limit the number of individual packet filters for a session.

If you decide to go this route, you'll need to enable the packet filters shown in Table 7-1.

Table 7-1. Packet Filters for Distributed Quarantine Resources

TRAFFIC TYPE	SOURCE PORT	DESTINATION PORT	ALTERNATIVES
Notifier	n/a	TCP 7250	None.
DHCP	UDP 68	UDP 67	None.
DNS	n/a	UDP 53	You can also specify the IP address of any DNS server.
WINS	n/a	UDP 137	You can also specify the IP address of any WINS server.
HTTP	n/a	TCP 80	You can also specify the IP address of any web server.
NetBIOS	n/a	TCP 139	You can also specify the IP address of any file server.
Direct hosting	n/a	TCP 445	You can also specify the IP address of any file server.

You can also configure any other packet filters peculiar to your organization.

The other approach is to limit your quarantined resources to a particular IP subnet. This way, you just need one packet filter to quarantine traffic to a remote user, but you have to readdress machines and, in most cases, take them out of their existing service or buy new ones.

When you use this method, the packet filter requirements are much simpler. You simply need to open one for notifier traffic on destination TCP port 7250, and one for DHCP traffic on source UDP port 68 and destination IDP port 67. For all other traffic, you should open the address range of the dedicated quarantine resource subnet. And again, you can also configure any other packet filters peculiar to your organization.

Writing the Baseline Script

The next step is to actually write a baseline script that will be run on the client. This is really independent to your organization, but all scripts must run RQC.EXE if the baseline compliance check was successful and they should include the following parameters:

```
rqc ConnName TunnelConnName TCPPort Domain Username ScriptVersion
```

The switches and arguments are explained in the following list:

- The ConnName argument is the name of the connectoid on the remote machine, which is most often inherited from the dial-in profile variable %DialRasEntry%.

- The TunnelConnName argument is the name of the tunnel connectoid on the remote machine, which is most often inherited from the dial-in profile variable %TunnelRasEntry%.

- The TCPPort argument is, obviously, the port used by the notifier to send a success message. This default is 7250.

- The Domain argument is the Windows security domain name of the remote user, which is most often inherited from the dial-in profile variable %Domain%.

- The Username argument is, as you might guess, the username of the remote user, which is most often inherited from the dial-in profile %UserName%.

- The ScriptVersion argument is a text string that contains the script version that will be matched on the RRAS server. You can use any keyboard characters except /0 in a consecutive sequence.

Here is a sample batch file script:

```
@echo off

echo Your remote connection is %1
echo Your tunnel connection is %2
echo Your Windows domain is %3
echo Your username is %4

set MYSTATUS=

REM  Baselining checks begin here

REM  Verify Internet Connection Firewall is live.
REM  Set CHECKFIRE to 1-pass, 2-fail.
<insert your various commands to check the ICF>
REM  Verify virus checker installed and sig file up.
REM  CHECKVIRUS is 1-pass, 2-fail.
<insert various commands to verify the presence of AV software and sig file>
```

```
REM  Pass results to notifier or fail out with message to user.
if "%CHECKFIRE%" == "2" goto :NONCOMPLIANT
if "%CHECKVIRUS%" == "2" goto :NONCOMPLIANT


rqc.exe %1 %2 7250 %3 %4 Version1-0
REM These variables correspond to arguments and switches for RQC.EXE
REM %1 = %DialRasEntry%
REM %2 = %TunnelRasEntry%
REM RQS on backend listens on port 7250
REM %3 = %Domain%
REM %4 = %UserName%
REM The version of the baselining script is "Version1-0"


REM  Print out the status
if "%ERRORLEVEL%" == "0" (
       set ERRORMSG=Successful baseline check.
) else if "%ERRORLEVEL%" == "1" (
       set ERRORMSG=Can't contact the RRAS server at the corporate network.
Contact a system administrator.
) else if "%ERRORLEVEL%" == "2" (
       set ERRORMSG=Access is denied. Please install the Connection Manager
profile from http://location and attempt a connection again.
) else (
       set ERRORMSG=Unknown failure. You will remain in quarantine mode
until the session timeout is reached.
)
echo %ERRORMSG%
goto :EOF


:NONCOMPLIANT
echo
echo Your computer has failed a baseline check for updates on
echo your machine.  It is against corporate policy to allow out of
echo date machines to access the network remotely. Currently
echo you must have Internet Connection Firewall enabled and
echo an updated virus scanning software package with the
echo latest virus signature files. For information about how to
echo install or configure these components, surf to
echo http://location.
Echo You will be permitted to access only that location until
Echo your computer passes the baselining check.


:EOF
```

Of course, the batch file is simple. You can make it as complex as you like; you can even compile a special program, because the postconnect script option in CMAK allows you to run an .exe file.

Installing the Listening Components

The Remote Access Quarantine Agent service, known otherwise as RQS.EXE, must be installed on the Server 2003 machines that are accepting incoming calls using RRAS. RQS is found in the Windows Server 2003 Resource Kit Tools download, which you can find on the Microsoft website. Once you've run the installer for the tools, select the Command Shell option from the program group on the Start menu, and run RQS_SETUP /INSTALL from that shell. This batch file will copy the appropriate binaries to the WindowsRoot\System32\RAS folder on your system and modify the service and Registry settings so that the listener starts automatically when the server boots up.

NOTE *To remove RQS.EXE, type **RQS_SETUP/REMOVE** at a command prompt.*

There's a bit of manual intervention required, however. You need to specify the version string for the baseline script. The listener service will match the version reported by the remote computer to the value stored on the RRAS computer so you can make sure that the client is using the latest acceptable version of a script. To make this change manually after you've run RQS_SETUP from the Tools download, do the following:

1. Open the Registry Editor.

2. Navigate to the HKEY_LOCAL_MACHINE\System\CurrentControlSet\Services\Rqs key.

3. Right-click in the right pane, and select New String.

4. Name the string AllowedValue.

5. Double-click the new entry, and enter the string that refers to an acceptable version of the script.

Alternatively, you can modify the RQS_SETUP batch file, so this step can be automated for future deployments. Do the following:

1.   Open the RQS_SETUP.BAT file in Notepad.

2.   Select Find from the Edit menu.

3.   In Find What, enter **Version1\0,** and click OK. The text cursor should be
     on a line that says: REM REG ADD %ServicePath% /v AllowedSet /
     t REG_MULTI_SZ /d Version1\0Version1a\0Test.

4.   To add just one acceptable version, delete "REM" from the beginning of
     the line.

5.   Now, replace the text "Version1\0Version1a\0Test" with the script ver-
     sion string you want to be passed by RQC.EXE.

6.   If you want to add more than one acceptable version, replace the text
     "Version1\0Version1a\0Test" with the acceptable version strings, each
     separated by the "\0" line.

7.   Save the file, and then exit Notepad.

RQS is set as a dependency of RRAS. However, when RRAS is restarted, RQS
doesn't automatically restart, so you'll need to manually restart it if you ever stop
RRAS manually.

NOTE   *By default, RQS.EXE listens on TCP port 7250. To change
the default TCP port, navigate to the HKEY_LOCAL_MACHINE\
SYSTEM\CurrentControlSet\Services\rqs\ key, create a new
REG_DWORD value called Port, and set it to the desired port.*

Creating a Quarantined Connection Profile

The next step is to create a quarantined Connection Manager profile, which happens to be a plain-vanilla profile with a few modifications. For one, you need to
add a postconnect action so that your baseline script will run and return a success or failure message to the RRAS machine. You also need to add the notifier to
the profile.

   In this section, I'll assume you're familiar with creating custom connectoids
with the Connection Manager Administration Kit (CMAK) wizard, because the
whole process is beyond the scope of this chapter and this book. The process

begins to differ at the Custom Actions screen (shown in Figure 7-1), so I'll begin this procedural outline there:

1. Navigate to the Custom Actions screen, and fill in subsequent screens as appropriate.

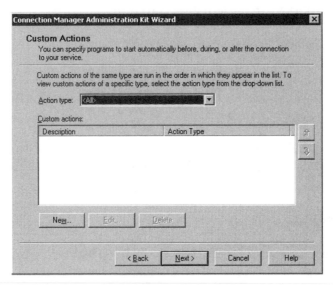

Figure 7-1. The Custom Actions screen of the CMAK wizard

2. Select Post-Connect from the Action type drop-down list, and then click the New button to add an action.

3. The New Custom Action dialog box is displayed, as shown in Figure 7-2.

4. Type a descriptive title for the postconnection action in the Description box. In Program to Run, enter the name of your baseline script. You can also use the Browse button to look for it. Type the command-line switches and their arguments in the Parameters box. Finally, check the two bottom boxes, Include the Custom Action Program with This Service Profile and Program Interacts with the User.

5. Click OK, and you should return to the Custom Actions screen. Click Next.

6. Continue filling in the wizard screens as appropriate, until you come to the Additional Files screen, as depicted in Figure 7-3.

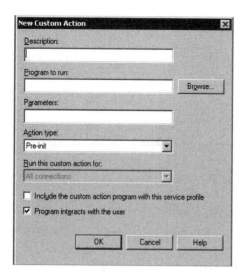

Figure 7-2. The New Custom Action dialog box

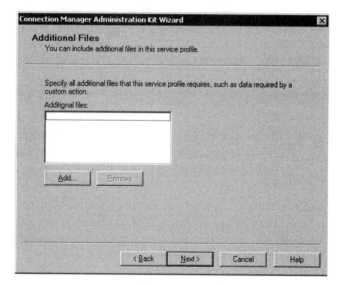

Figure 7-3. The CMAK wizard Additional Files screen

7. Click Add, and then enter RQC.EXE in the dialog box. You can use the Browse button to search for it graphically. Once you're finished, click OK.

8. You'll be returned to the Additional Files screen, where you'll see RQC.EXE listed. Click Next.

9. Complete the remainder of the wizard as appropriate.

Distributing the Profile to Remote Users

The profile you created earlier is made into an executable file that can be distributed to your remote users and run on their systems automatically. This creates a profile without any intervention after that. There are several options for actually getting that executable file to your users.

You could transmit the executable file as an attachment to an email message, or better yet, make a link to the executable file hosted on a web server somewhere. In the email message, you could include instructions to run the file and use those new connectoids for all future remote access. You could also have the executable run as part of a logon or logoff script, but to do that, you'd need to either have your users log on through a dial-up connection, or wait until the mobile users returned to the home network and connected at the corporate campus to the network.

Regardless of which method you choose, if you want to initially transmit the profile installer to your users, then you should always place the latest version of the profile installer on a quarantined resource somewhere, so that client computers that don't pass your baseline script's compliancy checks can surf to a website and download the latest version without compromising the integrity of your network further.

Configuring the Quarantine Policy

The final step in this process is to configure the actual quarantine policy within RRAS. In this section, I'll create a quarantine policy within RRAS that assumes you've posted the profile installer on a web server that is functioning as a quarantined resource.

NOTE   *If RRAS is configured to use the Windows authentication provider, then RRAS uses Active Directory or an NT 4 domain (remember, the RRAS machine needs only to be running Server 2003; it doesn't need to belong to an Active Directory–based domain) to authenticate users and look at their account properties. If RRAS is configured to use RADIUS, then the RADIUS server must be a Server 2003 machine running Internet Authentication Service (IAS). Incidentally, IAS also uses Active Directory, which is an NT domain to authenticate users and look at their account properties.*

1. Open the RRAS Manager.

2. In the left pane, right-click Remote Access Policies, and then select New Remote Access Policy from the context menu. Click Next through the introductory pages.

3. The Policy Configuration Method page appears. Enter Quarantined VPN remote access connections for the name of this policy, as shown in Figure 7-4. Click Next when you've finished.

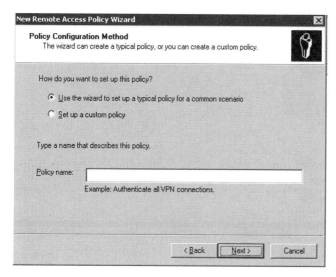

Figure 7-4. The Policy Configuration Method screen

4. The Access Method screen appears. Select VPN, and then click Next.

5. On the User or Group Access screen, select Group, and then click Add.

6. Type in the group names that should be allowed to VPN into your network. If all domain users have this ability, enter Everyone or Authenticated Users. I'll assume there's a group called VPNUsers on this domain that should have access to VPN capabilities. Click OK.

7. You'll be returned to the User or Group Access page, and you'll see the group name you added appear in the list box, as shown in Figure 7-5. Click Next if it looks accurate.

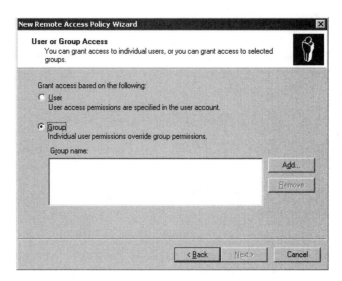

Figure 7-5. The User or Group Access screen

8. The Authentication Methods screen appears. To keep this example simple, use the MS-CHAP v2 authentication protocol, which is selected by default. Click Next.

9. On the Policy Encryption Level screen, make sure the Strongest Encryption setting is the only option checked, as shown in **Figure** 7-6. Then click Next.

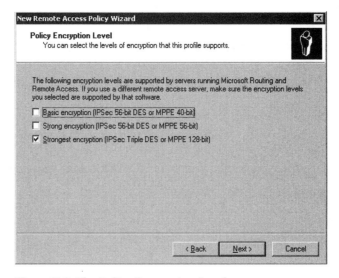

Figure 7-6. The Policy Encryption Level screen

10. Finish out the wizard by clicking Finish.

11. Back in RRAS Manager, right-click the new Quarantined VPN remote-access connections policy, and select Properties from the context menu.

12. Navigate to the Advanced tab, and click Add to include another attribute in the list.

13. The Add Attribute dialog box is displayed, as depicted in Figure 7-7.

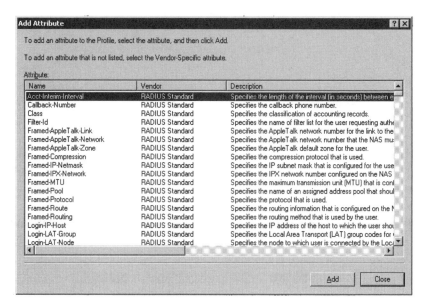

Figure 7-7: The Add Attribute dialog box

14. Click MS-Quarantine-Session-Timeout, and then click Add.

15. In the Attribute Information dialog box, type the quarantine session time in the Attribute Value field. Use a sample value of 60, which will be measured in seconds, for this demonstration. Click OK, and then OK again to return to the Advanced tab.

16. Click Add. In the Attribute list, click MS-Quarantine-IPFilter, and then click Add again. You'll see the IP Filter Attribute Information screen, as shown in Figure 7-8.

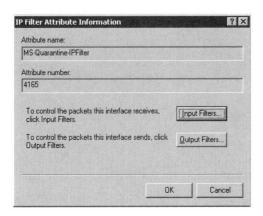

Figure 7-8. The IP Filter Attribute Information dialog box

17. Click the Input Filters button, which displays the Inbound Filters dialog box.

18. Click New to add the first filter. The Add IP Filter dialog box is displayed. In the Protocol field, select TCP. In the Destination port field, enter **7250**. Click OK.

19. Now, go back to the Inbound Filters screen, and select the Permit Only the Packets Listed Below option. Your screen should look like Figure 7-9.

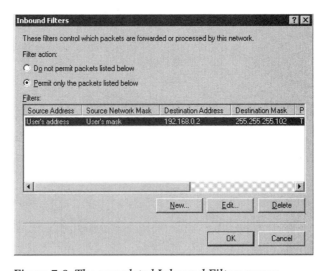

Figure 7-9. The completed Inbound Filters screen

20. Click New and add the input filter for DHCP traffic, and repeat the previous steps. Make sure to include the appropriate port number and type as described earlier in this chapter.

21. Click New and add the input filter for DNS traffic, and repeat the previous steps. Make sure to include the appropriate port number and type as described earlier in this chapter.

22. Click New and add the input filter for WINS traffic, and repeat the previous steps. Make sure to include the appropriate port number and type as described earlier in this chapter.

23. Click New and add an input filter for a quarantine resource, such as a web server, where your profile installer is located. Specify the appropriate IP address for the resource in the Destination Network part of the Add IP Filter screen, as shown in Figure 7-10.

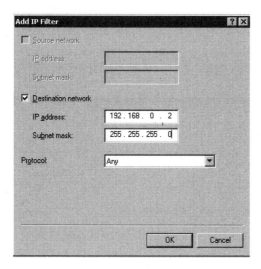

Figure 7-10. The Add IP Filter box, where you add a quarantined web resource

24. Finally, click OK on the Inbound Filters dialog box to save the filter list.

25. On the Edit Dial-in Profile dialog box, click OK to save the changes to the profile settings.

26. Then, to save the changes to the policy, click OK once more.

Creating Exceptions to the Rule

Although it's certainly advantageous to have all users connected through a quarantined session until you can verify their configurations, you may find some
logistical or political problems within your organization that mitigate this
requirement. If so, the simplest way to excuse a user or group of users from participating in the quarantine is to create an exception security group with Active
Directory. The members of this group should be the ones that need not partici-
pate in the quarantining procedure.

Using that group, you should create another policy that applies to the exceptions group, which is configured with the same settings as the quarantine
remote-access policy you created earlier in the chapter. This time, though, don't
add or configure either the MS-Quarantine-IPFilter or the MS-Quarantine-
Session-Timeout attributes. Once you've created the policy, move the policy that
applies to the exceptions group so that it's evaluated before the policy that quar-
antines everyone else.

Checkpoints

If you take nothing else from this chapter, note the following:

- Assess how much of a risk you're taking by not consistently and regularly
  verifying the update level of remote machines that connect to your
  network.

- Implement NAQC.

- Create exceptions groups for important people.

CHAPTER 8

Internet Information Services Security

EVER SINCE THE GARTNER REPORT came out in 2002, Microsoft's web platform has steadily deteriorated in reputation. That report advised anyone using Internet Information Services in any version as a public-facing, production web server to immediately consider switching to Apache, the popular UNIX web server. Most of it was deserved, too, when you consider the inexcusable buffer overflows, what seems like ten security bulletins each week, worms that take over computers faster than they can be secured when you're on the network, and so on.

Part of the problem was that the version of IIS included with Windows NT and Windows 2000, versions 4 and 5 respectively, were inexcusably lax in their default permissions: Everyone could do everything at any given time. Even the fact that IIS was installed by default during a Windows installation was a bad move: It didn't matter if you wanted a web server or not, because you got one anyway.

Those who prey on insecure web servers rely on users who are lax, lazy, or unknowledgeable about keeping their servers hardened and updated. Essentially, the climate of the Internet has degenerated into a situation where even innocent users that get penetrated are used as attack vectors against other innocent but open servers. The responsibility lies not just with the attackers who promulgate these worms, but with the administrators who allow their machines to be used like toys. The bottom line is this: If you can't keep your IIS server secure, you're the enemy, not a friend. Like the United States' recent Bush-era foreign policy, "If you're not with us, you're against us."

In this chapter, I'll look at nine simple steps you can take to make sure you're not a victim, and that you're not an accessory to the hackers. Note that entire books have been written about securely configuring IIS, and that's beyond the scope of this tome. But because IIS is bundled with Windows, I'll briefly look at ways you can easily harden IIS without having to purchase volumes of information.

Completely Disable IIS

Although it's probably the simplest suggestion in this section, it's also the most effective. It's a lot harder to attack a web server through a vulnerability in the web-server software when a machine isn't functioning as a web server. Unfortunately, Windows NT and Windows 2000 install IIS by default and enable it, too, so it's always running, or waiting to serve either a standard, legitimate HTTP request, or a message from a cracker.

IIS 6, found in Windows Server 2003, fixes this problem somewhat: When you first install Windows, IIS isn't enabled at all, and even when you do enable it, it starts in a locked-down mode whereby dynamic content generation and script-execution capabilities are disabled. You can only serve static HTML pages. This is a big step in the right direction. In fact, when you upgrade a machine running Windows 2000 Server to Server 2003, if it detects an IIS installation that still has the default settings engaged (a good sign it hasn't been modified or isn't in use), then it will disable IIS after the upgrade. You have to explicitly turn it back on.

If you do happen to be running IIS on a machine for any reason, and you'd like to decommission the machine as a web server, you can do so by following these steps:

1. Open the Computer Management applet inside Control Panel.

2. Double-click the Services icon to launch the Services console.

3. Scroll through the list and select World Wide Web Publishing Service.

4. Right-click the service, and select Stop.

5. Also, if you don't intend to run the web server anymore, set the startup options to Disabled, and the service won't be relaunched upon a reboot of the machine.

 TIP *You can also access the services with IIS Management, and from there, you can start and stop individual websites as well.*

Obviously, if you're actually using IIS, this suggestion won't help you, so let's continue to look at measures you can take to harden an IIS box.

Checking for Updates on Machines

Given the amount of patches released from 2001 to the present day, it can be tough to look at your network and determine the update level of each machine. Microsoft, sensing the need to remove a bit of egg from its face, purchased a license from Shavlik Technologies for the HFNetChk utility, short for Network Hotfix Checker. You can find hfnetchk.exe at the following location: `http://support.microsoft.com/default.aspx?scid=kb;en-us;303215` or at the famous Microsoft Knowledge Base in article number 303215.

NOTE *HFNetChk is exposed through the Microsoft Baseline Security Analyzer command-line interface through the following command: mbsacli.exe /hf. The latest version of the HFNetChk engine is available in MBSA v1.1.1.*

HFNetChk itself is a command-line tool that scans client computers for installed updates and patches. The comparison is based on an XML file of all available updates and the criteria for those updates, and the list is constantly updated by Microsoft.

The first time you run the tool, the tool will download the signed XML file, verify its authenticity, and decompress the file. HFNetChk then scans the selected computers to figure out the level of the operating system, service packs, and programs installed on the systems. HFNetChk looks at three aspects of your system to determine if a patch is installed: the Registry key that's installed by the patch, the file version, and the checksum for each file that's installed by the patch. By default, HFNetChk compares the files and Registry details on the computer that's being scanned to the XML file it downloads. If any of the three criteria discussed previously aren't satisfied, the tool considers the associated patch to be absent, and the results are displayed on the console. In the default configuration, HFNetChk output displays only those patches that are necessary to bring your computer up to date.

To use the tool, run the Microsoft Baseline Security Analyzer program and access HFNetChk from the command line with the –v option for verbose output, like this:

```
Mbsacli.exe /hf -v
```

The utility will scan your system and report back about what patches aren't present that should be. You can also scan with the following command:

```
mbsacli.exe /hf -d HASSELLTECH
```

This will specify that all computers in the NetBIOS domain name HASSELL-TECH should be scanned. It's a useful way to look at patch levels of multiple computers on the network at the same time.

Keeping IIS Updated

Now that you know what hotfixes you need, you can update all of your IIS boxes around your network. There are a few ways to do this, depending on how involved you as the administrator want to get. I'll look at two, with a tip for a third method.

Using Windows Update

Microsoft has recently improved its Windows Update website utility. When you surf to http://www.windowsupdate.com, the site will search your system to see what update level you're at, and then it will list which hotfixes and service packs would be applicable for your individual machine. This is a good yet automated way to ensure that all the code is completely up to date on your machine. The downside—you're never quite sure what's been installed where, because you don't actually go through the installation process yourself.

You can also set up the Automatic Updates utility in Windows by right-clicking My Computer and selecting Properties from the menu. Navigate to the Automatic Updates tab, and you can indicate to machines running Windows 2000 Server with at least Service Pack 3 or Windows Server 2003 if you want updates to automatically trickle down to your computer and be installed on a set schedule. If you set patches to automatically download and install, you won't ever have to worry about not being up to date. Alas, some people don't trust Microsoft enough to come out with robust patches that could simply be installed on the day of their release; most administrators are in the habit of waiting a few days after a patch and letting other businesses be guinea pigs. But if you're a one-person shop, and you have eight other tasks to do, the Automatic Updates solution might be good for you.

Using Network-Based Hotfix Installation

You can also download the individual security hotfixes and service packs one by one, save them to a central directory, and manually update each IIS machine on your network. Simply look at each security bulletin, or download the appropriate service packs (as of this writing, there are no service packs available for Windows Server 2003, but that will certainly change as time goes on), and store them in the same directory. Then, prepare a batch file.

Let's say you have two hotfix files to install. You surf the Web, find the files, and download them to \\mercury\qfe. Each hotfix is a separate executable. In order to simplify installation, I'll make use of two switches, –z and –m, that instruct the hotfix setup process to do so quietly (without raising dialog boxes to the user) and to avoid rebooting at the end. Armed with this knowledge, I'll simply prepare a batch file similar to the following:

```
Set qfedir=\\mercury\qfe\
%qfedir%Q554147_wxp_sp2.exe -z -m
%qfedir%Q711041_wxp_sp2.exe -z -m
```

Now, if you're running this batch file on computers running Windows 2000, you'll need to use the QChain utility. QChain looks at a group of updates you install, matches them up, reads their changes, and arranges them all so that you don't have to reboot after each hotfix installation. You invoke QChain after the hotfixes are installed, and it works its magic after that. So, we'll add the following line:

```
%qfedir%qchain.exe
```

Type that at the end of the previous batch file. Note that Windows XP and Server 2003 machines all have QChain functionality built in, so there's no need to run it.

I'll include all of that text in Notepad and save it as a file called UPDATE1.BAT. The first line sets a variable for the path to the hotfix files, and the variables are used in the lines that call each of the hotfixes. This way, if you decide to change the location of the hotfixes, you only have to update the first line, not each individual line.

Now, just run UPDATE1.BAT on all the computers that require those updates, or assign it via a login script through Group Policy.

TIP *If you deploy your Windows Server 2003 machines using Remote Installation Service (RIS), you can automatically preinstall all hotfixes before the actual Windows installation is complete, thereby saving you the time and tedium of applying them manually after Setup finishes. See any good book on Windows 2000 Server and Windows Server 2003 for more information on this.*

Securing Files, Folders, and Scripts

IIS has a bit of virtual-directory security, in that it has permissions for reading, writing, executing scripts, and other basic privileges within a virtual directory; these permissions are also independent of file-system permissions. Incidentally, this has been true for every version of IIS since its inception. Here's a reminder of the available rights:

- Script source access allows users to view the source code to scripts and applications within the selected directory, assuming that users have read or write permissions to that directory.

- Read access allows users to view or download files or directories, along with their individual properties.

- Write access allows users to upload files to the selected directory. It also allows them to change existing files within that directory.

- Directory browsing allows users to view an HTML page that lists the contents of the selected directory, including any subdirectories. Note that these subdirectories listed in this view are physical file-system directories, not IIS virtual directories.

To set these rights, use the IIS Manager, found under Administrative Tools inside Control Panel. Once the applet is launched, expand the computer tree in the left pane, and expand the node called Web Sites. All of the sites currently on that IIS machine are listed here. To set permissions, right-click the name of a site and choose Properties. Then, click the Home Directory tab, and you'll be greeted with a screen similar to that of Figure 8-1.

Figure 8-1. The IIS Manager Home Directory permissions section

On this page, you can make the necessary adjustments to permissions based on what content you have on each website. You can also follow the same procedure mentioned previously for each virtual directory on a website to further fine-tune the "virtual" permissions that IIS gives you.

But as I've mentioned earlier in the chapter, users browsing web content on your IIS machines are actually logging into a guestlike IUSR account on your machine or directory service. If they're using an account on the system, it logically follows that you can set permissions for that account on the file system to further reduce the chances of unauthorized access.

Out of the box, IIS 6 in Server 2003 sets the following restrictions on the NTFS permissions given to the IUSR account:

- A user logged on through the IUSR account can only read and list the contents of the web root directory. No execute permissions are present, so scripts cannot run, and no one can write files to the directory.

- The IUSR account has read, execute, and list contents permissions inside the Windows directory, just as the Authenticated Users group does.

Other than those exceptions, the IUSR account has no NTFS permissions across any file or folder on a disk. IIS 5, found in Windows 2000, conversely gives the IUSR account at least Read and sometimes Full Control rights over most objects on a disk. In both operating systems and IIS versions, you can use the NTFS permissions to lock down IUSR's ability to access content on your site even more.

The Microsoft Indexing Service

In Windows 2000, the Indexing Service is raring to go as soon as Setup finishes; the installation process for Server 2003 doesn't install the Indexing Service out of the box, so that ounce of prevention is a good step. However, no matter which operating system you're using, indexing files on your hard disk or network opens up a whole host of issues that may be difficult to see in foresight. For example, what if you indicate to the Indexing Service that you would like to index all files on your drive? The service would gladly do so, but it would also find angry letters to your users' superiors, love notes to their wives or girlfriends, salary information from the payroll department, memos from the boss on the latest round of layoffs, and so on. You can see that access to these bits of information by just anybody could create a disaster.

You can manage the Indexing Service using the Microsoft Management Console snap-in ciadv.msc. Loading the applet will present the dialog box shown in Figure 8-2.

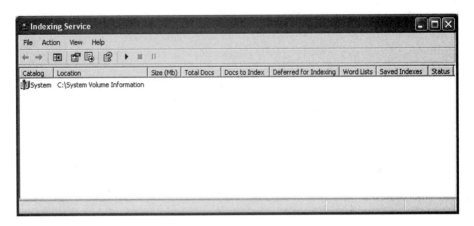

Figure 8-2. The Indexing Service management console

You can delete catalogs by simply right-clicking their name within the listing and selecting Delete. You can adjust the indexing properties for each catalog by right-clicking the name and selecting Properties. If you want the service NOT to index something, you can tell it directly (without the need for adjusting permissions) by right-clicking a catalog and selecting Directory from the New menu.

Now, bear with me for a moment as I delve into some seemingly backwards logic. The Indexing Service by default takes a directory and indexes all of its contents, including child files and subfolders. The key to excluding directories from indexing is to add a directory to the catalog and instruct the service not to index it. On the Add Directory dialog box, you see an option to the right, called Include in Index. This is where you can indicate whether or not to index a particular directory. So, you can enter the base directory for the index—let's call it C:\Documents—and tell the Indexing Service to index it by clicking Yes to the option on the right. But for this example, suppose you have a folder in C:\Documents called Top Secret. Tell Indexing Service to ignore it by adding C:\Documents\Top Secret as a directory, but before you click OK switch the Yes to a No under Include in Index.

Of course, that's a very backwards way of doing things, and it would have been a far better decision on the part of Microsoft to include an option that gives you the choice of which subfolders, if any, to index, within the management console of the Indexing Service. In true Microsoft form, you can make these changes somewhat intuitively, albeit in a different place—the Advanced Attributes section of the Properties sheet of any file or folder. Just right-click any folder, select Properties, and then go to the General tab and click Advanced. The top section, Archive and Index Attributes, contains an option that allows you to enable or disable the Indexing Service's access to this object. When you make a change and click OK, a dialog box will appear, asking if you want to apply the changes to subfolders and files within those subfolders.

With those points out of the way, consider the following suggestions for toning down the Indexing Service's influence in your organization.

- Immediately remove the two catalogs the service creates upon installation by default, called Web and System. These index all web content and all files on your system, respectively.

- Understand the hierarchical nature of the indexing permission. If you give a main folder permission to be indexed, any subfolders contained within that folder will automatically have permission to be indexed as well.

- Take the policy of blanket-disabling the indexing permission on folders, and explicitly enable the permission on files and folders that you're sure you want indexed. It's easier to control what's being indexed when everything is NOT indexed by default.

The Indexing Service is a good thing, when kept under control. Unfortunately, a few worms have decided to take advantage of some flaws in its construction, so if you make use of the service, you need to especially ensure that you keep your IIS machines updated early and often.

TCP/IP Port Evaluation

This should really go without saying at this point in this text—this IS a hardening book, after all—but go ahead and protect your IIS machines—only allow traffic on ports 80 and 443. I know there are remote-administration features, and those are great for internal servers, but with the continued security flaws that IIS has had, why take a chance exposing what amounts to root access to the outside world? Kill everything but ports 80 and 443 into your IIS machine and rest a bit easier at night.

You can disable these ports through a hardware or software firewall, or through an IPsec filter. I'll cover the IPsec method here, and this procedure will work for Windows 2000, Windows XP, and Windows Server 2003.

First, you need to create a filter action that describes what to allow and what to deny:

1. Start the Local Security Policy Microsoft Management Console (MMC) snap-in—you can do this from within Control Panel and Administrative Tools.

2. Right-click IPSec Security Policies on Local Machine, and then select Manage IP filter lists and filter actions.

3. Navigate to the Manage Filter Actions tab, and click Add to create a new filter action. Click Next to skip the introduction.

4. Type **LockDownWeb-Permit** as the name for the new filter action, because you'll be using this action to permit web traffic. Click Next when you're finished.

5. Select Permit, and then click Next.

6. Click Finish to complete the first filter action.

7. Create a second filter action called **LockDownWeb-Block** using the same procedure, except choose Block on the Filter Action dialog box this time.

8. Click Close once you're finished.

Now it's time to actually create the filters and lists based on the actions you defined previously:

1. Right-click IPSec Security Policies on Local Machine, and then select Manage IP Filter Lists and Filter Actions.

2. Click the Add button to create a new IP filter list.

3. Use **AllTraffic** for the filter list name.

4. Now, click the Add button again to create a new filter. Just select the default options through the IP Filter wizard to create a filter that will catch all traffic.

5. Click Close when you're finished.

6. Now, click Add to create another filter list, and use **CatchWebTraffic** for the name.

7. Click Add, and then click Next.

8. Select Any IP Address from the Source address drop-down list, and then click Next.

9. Select My IP Address from the Destination address drop-down list, and then click Next.

10. Choose TCP from the Select a Protocol Type drop-down list, and then click Next.

11. Select To This Port and then indicate port 80.

12. Click Next and then Finish.

At this point, you've filtered all traffic except for what's flowing to port 80. If you have an SSL site that needs access, click Add, and then repeat the second procedure to create another filter that permits traffic to go to port 443. You might want to make a note of the values presented in Table 8-1.

Table 8-1. Values to Create IPsec Rule for SSL Web Serving

PROMPT	INFORMATION
Source Address	Any IP address
Destination Address	My IP address
Protocol	TCP
From Port	Any
To Port	443

Administrative and Default Pages

Lots of web-based programs often come with sample files, instruction pages, and installation scripts that assist you in setting up and using the programs easily. In my web-hosting business, more than 75 percent of the scripts I use on a day-to-day basis, whether they're ones that my customers need installed or ones that I use to manage the systems, come with install scripts and default pages that leave access to an account, a database, or even worse—a machine—that's practically unguarded. These scripts don't advertise their presence, but it isn't hard for a nefarious cracker to look in standard places, like a directory called INSTALL, off the web root, and wreak havoc on a machine.

IIS is no different than these other programs. Here's an action list of items of which to rid yourself, assuming none are being actively used:

- IIS 6, found in Windows Server 2003, comes with a web-based program so that you can remotely administer an IIS server from afar. I'll make my comment on that in as few words as possible: bad idea.

- FrontPage Extensions also expose a lot of functionality that might not otherwise be needed. If you're using FrontPage, then by all means continue to make use of the bots, but if you've just installed the extensions because you don't feel like digging the Windows CD out if you ever need it again, then go ahead and uninstall it.

- Also, if you aren't using the extensions or any type of SharePoint site, be it from Team Services or the full-fledged Portal Server product, delete the Microsoft SharePoint Administration site.

- Get rid of web-based printing—does anyone actually use it anyway?—by deleting the folder called Printers from the web root.

The Ins and Outs of Internet Services Application Programming Interface

ISAPI is CGI's like-minded brother on the Windows platform. It allows for dynamic extensions to static HTML content, and new technologies like Active Server Pages and other dynamic languages use ISAPI filters to interact with IIS. Of course, this opens up a potential security hole.

You need to make sure that the only ISAPI filters configured on your system are those that are in use. (You can find ISAPI filters in the Properties sheet for any website.) For most systems, that would be the ASP.NET service. Look through your web root directory, and note the extensions on all of your content. Are there any that differ from .HTM? If not, make sure any filters that are listed in the Properties tab are removed.

As a colleague of mine points out, the entire Code Red virus could have been prevented had the IDA ISAPI filter been removed from IIS installations worldwide.

Looking at Apache as an Alternative

Of course, the best way to harden IIS may be to use Apache. You might be trading one headache for another, but let's look at some of the benefits that Apache offers over IIS.

Apache's model uses a parent and child process, whereby the parent only exists to make sure a child process is available. (In IIS 6 there's a similar model, but in previous versions there isn't.)

While IIS 6 has moved quite a lot of web serving down into the kernel to speed up requests and improve reliability, that might not be the best idea. Generally, the more you put in the kernel, the greater chance your operating system will fail.

Apache is also easy to modify, extend, and embrace. If you need a specific application platform, or a script, or something that doesn't come "in the box" per se, there's a good probability that with Apache's large user base, someone has already done it and made the results public.

Security is definitely a big issue. There will always be viruses and worms that target IIS. Apache issues security warnings from time to time, but they're limited in scope and generally easy to remedy. If there's a security hole in Apache, often you can work around it with a code fix, or you can change your configuration to work around the problem.

Checkpoints

In this chapter, I've discussed quick ways to ensure that your IIS machine doesn't become a victim of crackers and worms. Here is the list of points by which you can harden IIS:

- If you're not running a web server on your Windows machine, disable IIS.

- Regularly check the level of updates for your IIS machines, particularly those on an automated update regimen, and ensure that they're receiving the patches that they need to stay secure.

- Apply hotfixes and service packs as soon as possible after they're released and have gone through sufficient crash testing.

- Secure your web content using both IIS server permissions and NTFS file-system permissions, not one or the other.

- Consider whether you need the indexing service, and disable it if it isn't absolutely critical to your web operation.

- Close any ports that don't absolutely need to be open.

- On a related note, install a firewall in front of any public-facing IIS servers unless it's absolutely impossible.

- Delete any default web pages and directories, especially administrative install scripts, that could be used to obtain full privileges on your machine.

- Only use ISAPI filters if you need them. Delete any unused filters that exist on the server.

- Consider using Apache for your Internet-facing servers and using only IIS internally.

CHAPTER 9

Exchange 2000 Server Security

ALTHOUGH THE FOCUS OF THIS BOOK is on hardening the Windows client operating systems, so many organizations tend to install Windows servers for the purposes of running Exchange Server. So, respecting that fact, I decided to include a chapter on ways to very simply but effectively protect your Microsoft Exchange Server.

This is certainly not meant to be a complete guide—that could take an entire volume—but it's mentioned in this book to bring it to your attention, and to help you out in one of the most common administrative situations there is for Windows administrators.

Please note that this chapter primarily covers Exchange 2000 Server. Although Exchange Server 2003 was just released, most organizations are tending to hold off on its deployment, and instead are opting to refine their existing Exchange 2000 installations. I've made an attempt to note resources and tips that pertain to Exchange 2003 in this chapter, but do be aware that the focus is on the previous version. For a detailed site on configuring Exchange 2003 securely, please visit http://support.microsoft.com/default.aspx?scid=fh; en-us;exch2003.

 TIP *As an additional resource, Microsoft has a best practices document available at* http://www.microsoft.com/exchange/ techinfo/security/bestconfig.asp *that will give you more suggestions about applying security to Exchange 2000.*

Installation Security

There is, of course, a recommended way to install Exchange for the most versatility. Keep the following best practices in mind when installing Exchange on your network in the future:

- Install Exchange in its own Program Files directory on its own disk partition, separate from everything else.

- Place Exchange log files on their own partition, and place Exchange DB files on their own partition.

- After installation is complete, be sure to install the latest service packs for Exchange 2000. As of press time, the latest available release is Service Pack 3. Exchange 2003, because it has just been released, doesn't have any service packs available.

Set the following partition access control list (ACL) entries for each of the aforementioned partitions:

- For System, grant Full Control.

- For the local computer account, grant Full Control.

- For Domain Administrators, grant Full Control.

- For Authenticated Users, grant Read and Execute.

Additionally, you might consider creating an IPsec rule to protect the computer. In this ruleset, you might allow unrestricted use of the local network connection for domain users, other Exchange Server machines within your organization, and domain controllers. However, for others, consider limiting incoming traffic to port 80 for servers hosting Outlook Web Access (OWA) on Exchange. Block any other access.

NOTE   *The complete procedure for implementing IPsec rules is given in Chapter 8.*

Security Policy Modifications

Microsoft has made available baseline security guides, in the form of security templates, that you can apply as security policy according to the various roles your Exchange Server has. To apply them to your computers, you can simply import them into Group Policy via the Domain Group Policy or through a more granular object.

The Microsoft site with the security templates for Exchange Server machines is called the Security Operations Guide for Exchange 2000 Server and it's located at `http://www.microsoft.com/technet/treeview/default.asp?url=/technet/security/prodtech/mailexch/opsguide/e2ksec03.asp`.

NOTE   *Security templates are covered in depth in Chapter 3.*

In addition to the changes made by the previous templates, I would recommend that you make the modifications outlined in the following section.

For Exchange Server Machines

For the machines that run Exchange Server itself, I'd recommend these steps. Under User Rights Assignment, do the following:

- Grant the Access This Computer from the Network ability to the Authenticated Users, Backup Operators, and Enterprise Domain Controllers groups.

- Grant the Manage Auditing and Security Log ability to the Exchange Domain Servers group of your security domain.

Under Local Policies and Security Options:

- Set the value of Number of Previous Logons to Cache to 3.

- Disable the Shut Down System Immediately if Unable to Log Security Audits policy.

For Domain Controller Machines

For plain domain controllers, I'd recommend the following procedure. Under Local Policies and Security Options, do the following:

- Disable the Digitally Sign Client Communications (Always) policy.

- Disable the Digitally Sign Server Communications (Always) policy.

- Set the value of the LAN Manager Authentication Level policy to Send LM & NTLM—Use Ntlmv2 Session Security if Negotiated.

Service Security

Exchange runs as a set of services that communicate both within themselves and with the local computer. Additionally, the local computer and these processes act as a team when communicating with remote computers such as clients themselves, other Exchange servers within an organization, and Active Directory domain controllers.

Figure 9-1 shows the services that run on an Exchange server by default and the dependencies they have on each other and with other Windows server processes.

Exchange Server Service Dependencies

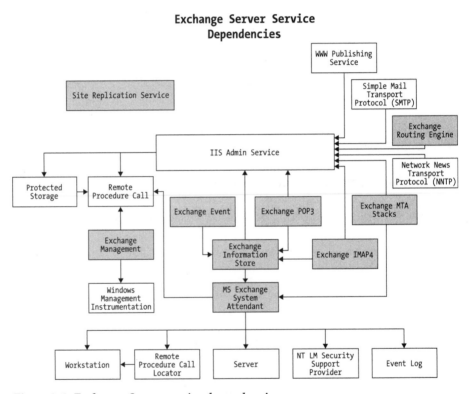

Figure 9-1. Exchange Server service dependencies

There are two classifications of Exchange servers. The front-end servers host OWA and are generally the machines that clients hit for data. The back-end servers hold the information store, mailboxes, public folder data, and other information and data repositories. Table 9-1 lists the recommended service states for a back-end Exchange 2000 Server machine.

Table 9-1. System Services for Exchange 2000 Machines

SERVICE	RECOMMENDED STATE
Iisadmin	Automatic
Imap4svc	Disabled
IPSEC Policy Agent	Automatic
Msexchangees	Disabled
Msexchangeis	Automatic
Msexchangemgmt	Automatic
Msexchangemta	Automatic
Msexchangesa	Automatic
Msexchangesrs	Disabled
Mssearch	Automatic
NTLM Security Support Provider	Automatic
POP3SVC	Disabled
Print Spooler	Disabled
Remote Procedure Call (RPC) Locator	Automatic
Resvc	Automatic
SMTPSVC	Automatic
Task Scheduler	Automatic
TermService	Automatic
W3SVC	Automatic
Windows Management Instrumentation	Automatic

Patch Management

To ensure that your Exchange Server machines stay as hardened and secure as possible during their duration in production, it's important to monitor security bulletins and keep up with the latest hotfixes and service packs. Remember that protecting Exchange is twofold: You need to patch Exchange, but you also need to patch the underlying operating system.

It so happens that vulnerabilities in Exchange 2000 don't happen as often as do general Windows operating-system vulnerabilities. However, because of this, the problems discovered in Exchange aren't usually publicized through Windows Update or Software Update Services, as described elsewhere in this book. Although this is slated to change in future releases of these tools—part of Microsoft's grand plan is to make patching all Microsoft products a one-stop affair—for now, it necessitates your subscribing to mailing lists and staying on top of issues. You can also make use of the Microsoft Baseline Security Analyzer, covered elsewhere in this book, to ensure that your system meets a secure configuration foundation.

Protecting Against Address Spoofing

A prominent way of intruding on any email system is by manipulating the From field in an email message. The Simple Mail Transfer Protocol (SMTP) doesn't verify a user's identity as presented in an email message, but Exchange can help you minimize this practice, which is commonly known as "message spoofing."

Perhaps the most nefarious problems related to address spoofing are external attackers who mimic an email address of an internal user. This social-engineering technique is used most often to encourage another user to disclose personal or sensitive information. Once the attacker has this data, he uses it to mount a more formal, sophisticated intrusion or attack. To make matters worse, Exchange 2000 will automatically resolve an email address in its address book to the name used in the global address list, which makes it quite difficult to discern a message's origin. Did it come from inside, or is it an Internet message? Fortunately, you can change Exchange's default configuration so that mail from outside the organization always remains unresolved, whether or not it contains a properly formatted address that matches one in the global address list. Then, instruct your users to look for unresolved email addresses as a warning sign of a spoofed message.

To set this behavior, do the following:

1. Start the Windows Registry Editor.

2. Locate or create the following key in the Registry (where *2* is the SMTP virtual server number): HKEY_LOCAL_MACHINE\SYSTEM\ CurrentControlSet\Services\MsExchangeTransport\Parameters\2.

3. Select Add Value from the Edit menu.

4. Add a value named ResolveP2, of type REG_DWORD.

5. To determine the value that you want to use, add the values for all of the elements that you want to be resolved, according to the key shown in Table 9-2.

Table 9-2. Values for the ResolveP2 key

FIELD	VALUE
From	2
To and CC	16
Reply to	32

For example, to resolve only the recipients, type only **16,** but to resolve From addresses and recipients, enter **18.**

6. Quit Registry Editor.

7. Restart the SMTP virtual server that you specified in step 2.

Use careful consideration when you select the servers that you want to enable this setting on. If you change the behavior on the default SMTP virtual server (generally virtual server instance 1, except on a cluster) and there are multiple servers, all internal mail that originates on other Exchange 2000 servers is also affected. Therefore, you may want to create a new SMTP virtual server, or only apply this setting on an incoming SMTP bridgehead server, because Exchange 2000 uses SMTP to route internal mail between servers.

An additional line of protection is available if you're receiving Internet email directly. You can configure your SMTP virtual server to perform a reverse DNS lookup on incoming email messages. This process verifies that the IP address of the transmitting SMTP server corresponds to the domain name listed in the message, an additional layer of SMTP security. However, the process is rather expensive in terms of processing power and message transmission latency.

To enable RDNS lookups, do the following:

1. Open Exchange System Manager.

2. Click Servers, and then navigate to the Exchange Server computer that you want to configure.

3. Expand Protocols and then SMTP.

4. Right-click Default SMTP Virtual Server, and then choose Properties from the context menu.

5. Navigate to the Delivery tab.

6. Click the Advanced button, and then click the Perform Reverse DNS Lookup on Incoming Messages checkbox.

7. Click OK, and then click OK again.

Protecting Against Denial-of-Service Attacks

Denial-of-service (DOS) attacks are generally very difficult targets from which to protect yourself. There are a couple of options within Exchange, however, that will help you to lessen the effect of them.

The message limits parameters allow you to configure a limit to the number of recipients per message as well as a maximum message size, a maximum number of messages per connection, and so on. These limits will help to ensure that a denial-of-service attack using mail transport is very difficult.

1. Open Exchange System Manager.

2. Click Servers, and then navigate to the Exchange Server computer that you want to configure.

3. Expand Protocols and then SMTP.

4. Right-click Default SMTP Virtual Server, and then choose Properties from the context menu.

5. Navigate to the Messages tab.

6. To set a maximum message size, click the Limit Message Size to (KB) box and enter a value in the Size box.

7. To set a maximum size on a particular SMTP session, click the Limit Session Size to (KB) box, and enter a value.

8. To set a maximum number of messages per connection (the default is 20), click the Limit Number of Messages per Connection box and then enter a value.

9. To set a maximum number of recipients for a single message, click the Limit Number of Recipients per Message box and enter a value. Any messages that are larger than this number of recipients is returned to the sender with a nondelivery report (NDR)—commonly known as a bounce message.

10. Click OK.

An attacker could also poison your Exchange machines by sending a large number of mails to a particular server until it runs out of disk space to store them. You can prevent the negative effects of this by setting storage limits on mailboxes and public folders, as follows:

1. In Exchange System Manager, expand the Servers container.

2. Select the server that hosts the mailbox store that you want to configure, and then double-click Storage group in the right pane.

3. Right-click the mailbox store that you want to configure, select Properties, and navigate to the Limits tab.

4. Click to select one or all of the following checkboxes under Storage limits:

    • To simply warn a user that his mailbox has exceeded its limit, click Issue Warning At. Type a value in kilobytes.

    • To send a warning message that states that the user will not be able to send any more messages until she deletes or archives her old mail, select Prohibit Send At. Type a value in kilobytes.

    • To send a warning message that states that the user has exceeded mailbox limits and cannot receive any messages, select Prohibit Send and Receive At. Type a value in kilobytes.

5. Either click the time that you want the warning messages to be generated in the Warning Message Interval box or click Customize to select times from a calendar.

6. After you configure the warning message interval times, click OK.

Restricting SMTP Access

SMTP is one of the most insecure protocols around, and that's not a good thing to have coming into a server system that contains some of the most sensitive information in your organization. Fortunately, you have some manner of control over this. There are several options in the properties of the SMTP Virtual Server on an Exchange 2000 Server computer that can be used to restrict SMTP privileges and access. To see them, navigate to the Access tab on the Default SMTP Virtual Server Properties dialog box, as shown in Figure 9-2.

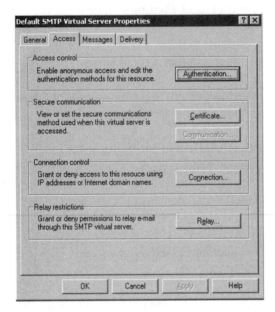

Figure 9-2. The SMTP Virtual Server Properties Access tab

Click the Edit button under the Access Control section of the tab. You'll see a dialog box called Authentication Methods. Anonymous access to your SMTP server is enabled here by default. In the bottom portion of the box, you can specify the method by which nonanonymous users will authenticate. The first option is basic authentication, which negotiates a username and password in clear text between the client and the SMTP server. There's also Integrated Windows Authentication, which encrypts the username and password and sends it between the client and the server. This uses either the SAM accounts database on the IIS server machine or Windows' built-in integration with Active Directory. Finally, there's SSL authentication, which uses certificates only to establish the identity of a client to a server. Either of the latter two options will work if you want credentials to be passed in a secure environment; basic authentication simply passes the credentials over the wire unprotected, leaving an open door for sniffers.

Back on the Access tab, you can grant or deny access to a site based on the client's IP address. This is useful if you have an abusive group of hosts that perhaps have been cracked, or if you wish to restrict users of a site to only internal hosts. Click the Edit button under IP Address and Domain Name Restrictions to configure this. You first select whether all users will be granted or denied access to the site by using the radio buttons at the top of the window. Then, you can configure individual exceptions to the rule you defined previously in the White List box. Click Add to include an address in the Exceptions list. You'll be prompted with a box, asking whether you'd like to except a single computer, a group of computers (an IP subnet), or an entire domain (DNS-based domain, that is). Again, restricting or allowing access based on a DNS domain name is a very expensive operation, because each HTTP request must be accompanied by a reverse lookup on the part of the IIS server. This can slow response time considerably and cause processor utilization to increase significantly. Enable this only if you're sure of the consequences or if you have a relatively lightly traveled website to restrict.

Select the appropriate response, and then type in the actual IP address, network number and subnet, or domain name. You can click the DNS Lookup button to perform a reverse lookup on a certain domain name in order to obtain its appropriate IP numbers. When you're finished, click OK, and you'll be returned to the Restrictions dialog box. Now, keep in mind that if you've configured default access for everyone to your site, the excepted addresses will be denied access. Conversely, if you've denied access by default to all IP addresses, the excepted addresses will be allowed access. This may seem obvious, but during a quick change it's easy to become a little confused at the quasi-backward logic. Click OK once you're finished.

Finally, the Relay Restrictions section of the Access tab lets you lock down your server so that it can be used only by clients that you've approved of and not by anonymous spammers that could take advantage of your open resource. This functions similarly to the Connection Control dialog box, where you add IP addresses and allow or deny their access to the server. The difference is that with a relay restriction, you're only saying that these IP address aren't allowed to send outgoing mail through this server. With the connection control, you're restricting the ability of a set of addresses to even communicate with the server—either to bring mail to the server OR to send outgoing mail. This is an important distinction.

Usually, you add local IP addresses on your site to this list and only allow those addresses to talk. Also, you can specify whether computers that authenticate to the SMTP server can send outgoing email, regardless of whether they appear in the list. This is useful for Internet addresses—your clients, as long as they authenticate, can still use the SMTP server even though their address isn't local.

Controlling Access

Exchange 2000 uses administrative groups, which are collections of Exchange 2000 objects that are grouped together to help manage and delegate permissions. An administrative group can contain policies, routing groups, public folder hierarchies, servers, conferencing objects, and chat networks.

The easiest way to assign permissions to administrative groups is through the Exchange Administration Delegation wizard, which requires a user with Full Control over the Exchange organization. To start the Exchange Administration Delegation wizard, right-click the organization or administrative group in Exchange System Manager, and then select Delegate Control from the context menu.

Table 9-3 shows the three administrative roles provided in Exchange 2000.

Table 9-3. Administrative Roles in Exchange 2000

ROLE	DESCRIPTION
Exchange View Only	Can list and read properties of all objects in child containers.
Exchange Administrator	Can do all administrative tasks and grant all permissions except taking ownership, changing permissions, or opening user mailboxes.
Exchange Full Administrator	Can do all administrative tasks and grant all permissions except opening user mailboxes or impersonating a user's mailbox.

In some cases you'll find that using the Exchange Administration Delegation wizard doesn't provide enough granularity in assigning security. You can modify the Security tab on the individual objects within Exchange. However, by default, the Security tab is only displayed on address lists, global address lists, mailbox stores, public folder stores, and the top-level public folder hierarchy. To display the Security tab on all Exchange objects, you need to make a Registry change, as follows:

1. Run the Registry Editor.

2. Locate the following key in the registry: HKEY_CURRENT_USER\ Software\Microsoft\Exchange\ExAdmin.

3. Select Add Value from the Edit menu.

4. Add a value named ShowSecurityPage, of type REG_DWORD.

5. Double-click the new value, and enter a **1** for its attribute.

This change takes effect immediately, so you don't need to restart Exchange System Manager. However, the change will only affect the user that's currently logged on.

Checkpoints

In this chapter, I've looked briefly at the high points of hardening Exchange 2000 Server and its environment. The strategies I recommend include the following:

*   Install Exchange in its own Program Files directory on its own disk partition, separate from everything else.

*   Place Exchange log files on their own partition, and place Exchange DB files on their own partition.

*   After installation is complete, be sure to install the latest service packs for Exchange 2000. As of press time, the latest available release is Service Pack 3.

*   Set the following partition access control list (ACL) entries for each of the aforementioned partitions as defined in the chapter.

*   Consider creating an IPsec rule to protect Exchange Server computers.

*   Use the baseline security templates from Microsoft's Security Operations Guide for Exchange 2000 Server site in order to implement policy-based security.

*   Make the outlined policy changes in this chapter in addition to the previous baseline templates so you can harden your system even more.

*   Understand the dependencies of Exchange Server and general Windows operating-system services.

*   Make the appropriate changes to service state as suggested in this chapter.

*   Stay on top of security hotfixes and service releases for not only Exchange Server, but Windows server versions as well.

- Subscribe to a security bulletin mailing list.

- Set Exchange to not resolve Internet email messages, so that your users can easily detect a spoofed message.

- Enable reverse DNS lookups on Internet mail received so that you can verify the transmitting SMTP server's identity and the trustworthiness of a particular message.

- Set a maximum number of recipients per message.

- Set a maximum message size.

- Set a maximum number of messages per SMTP session.

- Set a maximum size of an SMTP session.

- Set storage limits on mailboxes and public folders so you can prevent an attacker from filling up disk space.

- Restrict SMTP access by IP address or domain.

- Ensure that your SMTP server is a closed relay so you can prevent spammers from taking advantage of your connection.

- Delegate Exchange permissions appropriately.

- Modify Exchange System Manager so that the Security tab is present in the Properties view of all objects.

CHAPTER 10

Security Auditing and Event Logs

YOU'VE COME TO THE FINAL CHAPTER in this book, which is no small feat—congratulations! This part of the book focuses mainly on how you can discern if your hardening efforts, fine-tuned with what you've learned in the first nine chapters, were successful at thwarting attacks. Event logs and security auditing policies are an astute administrator's best friend, but most IT personnel overlook logs, as if logs were there for no other purpose than to simply take up valuable hard disk space.

Auditing and event-viewing procedures are different on Windows NT, 2000, XP, and Server 2003, so I'll group each platform and tackle different approaches independently. At the close of the chapter, I'll look at ways to decipher events and make log searching and checking easier.

For Windows 2000, XP, and Server 2003

Auditing controls and properties for versions of Windows later than NT are modified through Group Policy objects (GPOs) in Windows 2000, XP, and Server 2003. Assuming your computer is participating in an Active Directory domain, you can find the domain auditing policy inside the Default Domain Policy, by selecting Computer Configuration ➤ Windows Settings ➤ Security Settings ➤ Local Policies ➤ Audit Policies. Otherwise, you can view the Local Security Policy through the Administrative Tools applet in Control Panel.

The settings for each Group Policy object indicate on what type of events and on what type of result a log entry will be written. The options for auditing policies are outlined here:

- Audit account logon events

- Audit account management

- Audit directory service access

- Audit logon events

- Audit object access

- Audit policy change

- Audit privilege use

- Audit process tracking

- Audit system events

You can configure individual objects to be audited by editing the System Access Control List (SACL) for any given object, which is much like assigning permissions, except that it's indicating to Windows on what type of access an event log entry should be writing. You can access the SACL for an object by clicking the Advanced button on the Security tab of its properties sheet. On the Auditing tab, you can click Add to include new auditing events for an object, or click View ➤ Edit to modify an existing auditing event. Figure 10-1 shows the SACL for an object.

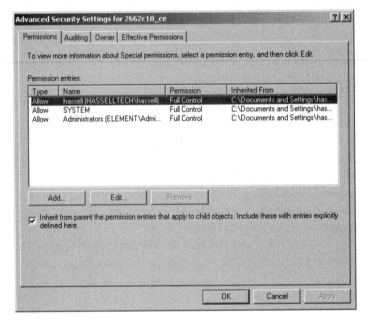

Figure 10-1. The SACL for an object

 NOTE *Only NTFS files and folders can be audited. FAT partitions don't support auditing events because they don't contain the necessary permission information.*

Recommended Items to Audit

You'll want to take particular note of the following items from your event logs:

- Logon and logoff events, which can indicate repeated logon failures and point to a particular user account that's being used for an attack

- Account management, which indicates users who have tried to use or have used their granted user- and computer-administration power

- Startup and shutdown, which shows both the user who has tried to shut down a system and what services may not have started up properly upon the reboot

- Policy changes, which can indicate the users who are tampering with security settings

- Privilege use, which can show any attempts to change permissions to certain objects

Event Logs

Similarly to auditing policies, the policies for configuring the event logs are found inside the Default Domain Policy, by selecting Computer Configuration ➤ Windows Settings ➤ Security Settings ➤ Local Policies ➤ Event Log.

The settings for each of these GPOs indicate the amount of disk space dedicated to storing log events as well as the permissions granted to view the event logs, how long their contents are retained before rolling over to new logs, and how those event logs are supposed to be retained during that time. The options for event-log policies are described here:

- Maximum application log size

- Maximum security log size

- Maximum system log size

- Restrict guest access to application log

- Restrict guest access to security log

- Restrict guest access to system log

- Retain application log

- Retain security log

- Retain system log

- Retention method for application log

- Retention method for security log

- Retention method for system log

- Shut down the computer when the security audit log is full

The Event Viewer

The Event Viewer allows you to look at events in three event logs. Figure 10-2 shows a typical Event Viewer console.

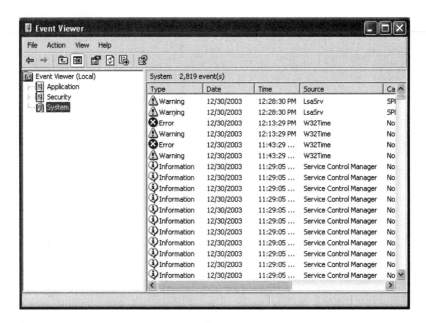

Figure 10-2. An Event Viewer console

First, the security log displays successes and failures with regard to privilege use, and classifies them into categories such as object access, account logon, policy change, privilege use, directory service access, and account management. The remaining event logs have three different classes of entries: errors, informational events, and warnings. The application log consists of information reported from programs running on the system. The system log consists of events and exceptions thrown by Windows itself. All users can see the system and application logs, but only members of the administrators group can see the security log.

To clear all events from your Event Viewer console, choose Clear All Events from the Action menu.

For Windows NT 4.0

Auditing is a necessary part of Windows NT's C2 security certification, but it's not enabled by default. You'll need to enable it on each NT machine by opening the User Manager and selecting Audit from the Policies menu. You'll be presented with an Audit Policy dialog box, as shown in Figure 10-3.

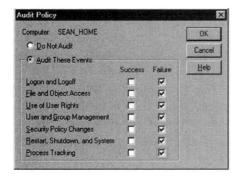

Figure 10-3. The NT Audit Policy dialog box

How you configure the auditing policy depends on how detailed you want to get in your log reviews. If you're simply interested in looking out for suspicious and possibly nefarious activity, then you should restrict your auditing events to a few serious classes of events and of those, only failure events. If, however, forensic analysis is your hobby, you may want to log everything possible, so you can extract as complete a picture as possible of a sequence of events that may require later investigation.

To turn on auditing of specific objects, you can click the Auditing button on the Security tab of their properties sheet, as depicted in Figure 10-4.

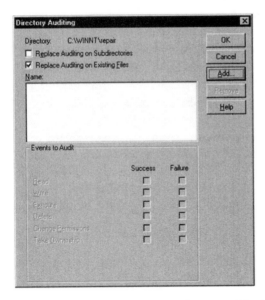

Figure 10-4. Enabling auditing for a specific object

Recommended Items to Audit

You'll want to take particular note of the following items from your event logs:

- Audit failures for logon and logoff events

- Audit all file and object-access events for files and directories of special interest or particular concern

- Audit failures of user rights

- Audit both successes and failures of user- and group-management privileges

- Audit both successes and failures of security policy changes—especially successes, because they would occur rarely in legitimate practice

- Audit failures in restart, shutdown, and system events

- Audit failures of process-tracking events

The Event Log

You can specify the retention policy, maximum log size, and rollover functions for each log from the Event Viewer application by selecting Start ➤ Programs and navigating to the Administrative Tools folder. From the Log menu, choose Log Settings. Select the log to configure in the Change settings for drop-down list, and then specify a maximum size for that particular log in kilobytes. You can also choose to overwrite older events when the maximum size is reached, overwrite events at Windows' discretion, or not to overwrite at all, which requires manual administrator intervention.

You can clear all events in a particular log by choosing Clear All Events from the Log menu of Event Viewer.

Filtering Events

In all versions of Windows, it's quite easy to limit the display of event items within Event Viewer to only those that match certain criteria. In Windows NT, select Filter Events from the View menu. In all other version of Windows, select Filter from the View menu. You'll see a dialog box much like Figure 10-5.

Figure 10-5. Filtering in the Event Viewer application

From this dialog box, you can indicate the events that interest you in a variety of ways, including by date (the From and To fields), success or failure (the checkboxes in the Event Types area), the class of the event (the Category drop-down list), the affected user, the system where the event originates, and the event type.

TIP *You can obtain a translation of a specific event ID number at* http://www.eventid.net. *You can enter the ID number and obtain a helpful explanation of the event, what it might mean, and the operating systems that it affects.*

What Might Be Missing

If you're reconstructing an occurrence through event logs, you might scratch your head at the absence of some events from any of your logs. This section offers a bit of explanation as to why that might be.

First, no audit events will be generated for unsuccessful attempts to access and modify a file or directory of interest if you haven't enabled security auditing for that item. To record such events, you have to enable auditing for the item. Also, I'll note once more that you can only audit items on NTFS file systems.

Second, failed login events in which the user has entered an invalid password aren't recorded in the audit logs for domain controllers in Active Directory or the primary domain controller in an NT 4 domain. Instead, those failed attempts are logged in the security log for the computer at which the failure occurred. Additionally, you must enable auditing on that system for the recording to occur.

TIP *There are some third-party software products that can help you manage auditing and event logs, including AuditPro from Network Intelligence India, at* http://www.nii.co.in/software/apwin.html, *and Informant from RippleTech, at* http://www.rippletech.com/products/Informant/Prod_INF_Overview.htm.

Checkpoints

In this final chapter you've learned how to use security auditing and event logs for various versions of Windows; these will support your hardening efforts. The key auditing strategies for this chapter for Windows 2000, XP, and Server 2003 users are as follows:

- Logon and logoff events, which can indicate repeated logon failures and point to a particular user account that's being used for an attack.

- Account management, which indicates users who have tried to use or used their granted-user and computer-administration power.

- Startup and shutdown, which displays both the user who has tried to shut down a system and what services may not have started up properly upon the reboot.

- Policy changes, which can indicate users tampering with security settings.

- Privilege use, which can show attempts to change permissions to certain objects.

For Windows NT users, the chief auditing points include the following:

- Audit failures for logon and logoff events.

- Audit all file and object access events for files and directories of special interest or particular concern.

- Audit failures of user rights.

- Audit both successes and failures of user- and group-management privileges.

- Audit both successes and failures of security policy changes—especially successes, because they would occur rarely in legitimate practice.

- Audit failures in restart, shutdown, and system events.

- Audit failures of process-tracking events.

For all versions of Windows, the following items apply:

- Make searching easier by filtering events inside Event Viewer.

- Search on events that interest you at http://www.eventid.net to learn more about them.

- Understand why some events might not be recorded in certain error logs.

Quick-Reference Checklists

FOR EASY REFERENCE AND USE, I've compiled the chapter checklists from each section of the book into one master list and placed it here in the appendix. The lists are separated by chapter, so you can easily look up the discussion around a particular point.

Chapter 1

- Learn the cornerstones of good security policy: privacy, trust, authentication, and integrity.

- Understand the social implications of security.

- Recognize the security dilemma—that users must understand the need for security and agree to the extent to which security is implemented.

- Consider transfers of trust in security policy.

- Understand the process of defining the concept of security: identification of the object to protect, evaluation of risk, and proposals for counter-measures to potential attacks.

- Recognize some of the enemies of a secure system: complexity, backward compatibility, backups.

- Embrace the role that hardening takes in protecting against unknown threats.

- Apply service packs to operating systems and applications throughout your company.

- Purchase, install, and keep updated antivirus software installed throughout your company networks.

- Test and scan new downloads, and practice safe computing when transferring files from public networks.

- Wipe virus-infected systems to a clean hard disk as soon as possible.

- Block malicious file attachments as they enter your network at the email server, before it reaches the client.

- Install a firewall and close off networking ports (TCP 135, 139, and 445; UDP 135, 137, and 445) and any other unused ports.

- Consider the purchase and installation of an intrusion detection system.

- Properly restrict access to remote entry points to your network, and encourage the use of virtual private networks over traditional telephonic and modem connections.

- Implement dial-back for standard plain telephone connections.

- Investigate physical segmentation of your network.

- Properly harden and secure any IIS systems on the network, and relegate IIS systems to a blocked-off segment of the network during the installation of patches.

- Read the rest of this book.

Chapter 2

- Use Windows NT System Policies and the included editor to set appropriately restrictive system policies for your organization.

- Set the maximum password age for your users to 90 days.

- Set the minimum password age for your users to 1 day.

- Set the minimum password length for your users to eight characters.

- Set the uniqueness factor for your passwords to at least five.

- Set the account lockout settings to five failed attempts and a counter reset after ten minutes.

- Change your NT/2000/XP passwords that contain only numbers and letters so that they also include at least one other nonalphanumeric character.

- Rename the administrator account carefully.

- Remove the Everyone group from ACLs and add the Authenticated Users group in its place.

- Disable the Guest account.

- Disable remote access and control of the Registry, or at the very minimum tightly control it.

- Disable the display of the username of the last person to have used the system.

- Set tight permissions on the security event log.

- Set tight permissions on printers and printer drivers, particularly those associated with certain sensitive roles, such as invoicing and check production.

- Disable anonymous logins, particularly their ability to list account names.

- Set tight permissions on the ability to set scheduled tasks, either via the Windows GUI or through the command-line AT tool.

- Secure local directories and assign restrictive permission to the Everyone or Authenticated Users group on those directories.

- Ensure that system directories come before anything else in the search path.

- Lock the operating-system directory down very securely.

- Use the included port-filtering utility to restrict network traffic to incoming ports on which legitimate business is conducted.

- Stay aware of new threats by subscribing to virus-related mailing lists.

- Purchase antivirus software specifically designed for NT, not just any software for "all versions of Windows."

- Configure your antivirus software to perform automatic virus-definition updates, preferably on a nightly or at least weekly basis.

- Pay considerable attention to the integrity of code and applications downloaded from the Internet.

- Install software as a un- or under-privileged user.

- Grant user rights only to those users who need it.

- Assign default user rights to appropriate groups, as detailed earlier in the chapter.

Chapter 3

- Update to the latest service-pack level for your platform.

- Create a "slipstreamed" distribution CD to deploy the latest service pack update to any new OS installs.

- Use the latest hotfix file patches from Microsoft to relieve your system of vulnerabilities.

- Download and use HFNetChk to scan and inventory your network for security patch installations.

- Set restrictions on Windows passwords. They should be at least six characters long, they shouldn't be based on a dictionary word, and they shouldn't last longer than 90 days.

- Configure Windows to disable, or "lock out" accounts, for at least 15 minutes after three unsuccessful authentication attempts.

- Disable all anonymous access except where explicitly allowed in file-system permissions.

- Disable the ability to shut down a system without first logging in to it.

- Enable automatic logoff upon logon time expiration, and set up at least one half hour each night where no user is permitted to log on.

- Require digitally signed communications when possible, but not always.

- Require the user to press Ctrl-Alt-Del before logging on, a key sequence recognized only by the Windows operating system.

- Do not permit the username of the last user to be displayed at logon.

- Remind users to change their password automatically at least 14 days before its expiration.

Chapter 4

- Use XP's included Internet Connection Firewall to close off open ports.

- Enable ICF logging for later forensic analysis and intrusion detection.

- If you have a small office or home office network, purchase an inexpensive broadband router for further protection.

- Adjust your running services list to match that in the book.

- Test your service load and ensure only services required for necessary functionality are running and enabled.

- Use the Microsoft Baseline Security Analyzer (MBSA) to analyze the current update level of machines on your network.

- Also visit Windows Update to identify and install appropriate hotfixes and software updates.

- Visit a reputable online software vendor and perform penetration tests on your machines to ensure that ports are closed off and your hardening efforts were effective.

- Format the partitions on your machines with NTFS.

- Disable automated logins by ensuring that there's a password for each user account on a machine. (This applies only to machines not participating in a security domain.)

- Rename the Administrator account.

- Rename the Guest account.

- Replace the Everyone group with the Authenticated Users group inside the access control lists (ACLs) of your shares.

- Understand the typical signs of a compromised machine.

- If a machine becomes compromised, don't attempt to resurrect it. Get personal data off, verify the integrity of that data, and then reformat and reinstall the machine.

Chapter 5

- Group your policies logically and define boundaries to contain them.

- Inside those boundaries, configure policies that represent common values in your organization.

- Configure organizational units inside Active Directory that contain machines grouped according to like roles, or functions within an organization.

- Adjust the default domain security policy to encompass a common security configuration to be deployed across all systems in your domain.

- Adjust the default domain controller security policy to more secure settings that should be applied to all machines serving that role in your Active Directory.

- Use the Computer Configuration nodes in Group Policy to adjust machine-specific settings regardless of the logged-on user.

- Use the User Configuration nodes in Group Policy to adjust user-specific settings that will follow the person across all machines in the policy's scope.

- Check your domain's DNS configuration to make sure SRV subrecords are being properly registered.

- Make sure that the No Override and Block Inheritance functionality of Group Policy isn't hindering the application of Group Policy objects.

- Examine your domain controller logs to see if the File Replication Service is throwing any errors related to versioning of GPT files.

- Force a refresh of Group Policy from a domain controller's command line if all else fails.

Chapter 6

- Don't do anything else until you have some sort of patch-management system installed and running on your network. It WILL BE a priority one of these days if your network is connected to the Internet.

- Deploy SUS unless you have a large business that would benefit from SMS, you're already running SMS, or you've already got a sufficient patch-management system in place.

- Set SUS to automatically synchronize on a daily basis, so that you receive updates as soon as possible after they are released.

- Approve only the updates for localizations that you maintain. There's no need to have the Japanese version of a patch if you have no Japanese-installed Windows machines.

- Use Group Policy or some other automated method to deploy the Automated Updates client to machines that aren't currently running at least Windows 2000 Service Pack 3 or Windows XP Service Pack 1.

- Enable Automatic Updates on your network.

- Schedule update installations at least weekly, if not daily.

- Educate your users about the ramifications of not keeping their systems updated.

- Use event-log monitoring software to ensure that SUS continues to function correctly.

- Did I mention that you shouldn't do anything else until you have some sort of patch-management system installed and working on your network?

Chapter 7

- Assess how much of a risk you're taking by not consistently and regularly verifying the update level of remote machines that connect to your network.

- Implement Network Access Quarantine Control (NAQC).

- Create exceptions groups for important people.

Chapter 8

- If you're not running a web server on your Windows machine, disable IIS.

- Regularly check the level of updates for your IIS machines, particularly those on an automated update regimen, and ensure that they're receiving the patches that they need to stay secure.

- Apply hotfixes and service packs as soon as possible after they're released and have gone through sufficient crash testing.

- Secure your web content using both IIS server permissions and NTFS file-system permissions, not one or the other.

- Consider whether you need the indexing service, and disable it if it isn't absolutely critical to your web operation.

- Close any ports that don't absolutely need to be open.

- On a related note, install a firewall in front of any public-facing IIS servers unless it's absolutely impossible.

- Delete any default web pages and directories, especially administrative install scripts, that could be used to obtain full privileges on your machine.

- Only use ISAPI filters if you need them. Delete any unused filters that exist on the server.

- Consider using Apache for your Internet-facing servers and only using IIS internally.

Chapter 9

- Install Exchange in its own Program Files directory on its own disk partition, separate from everything else.

- Place Exchange log files on their own partition, and place Exchange DB files on their own partition.

- After installation is complete, be sure to install the latest service packs for Exchange 2000. As of press time, the latest available release is Service Pack 3.

- Set the partition access control list (ACL) entries for each of the aforementioned partitions as defined in the chapter.

- Consider creating an IPsec rule to protect Exchange Server computers.

- Use the baseline security templates from Microsoft's Security Operations Guide for Exchange 2000 Server site in order to implement policy-based security.

- Make the outlined policy changes in this chapter in addition to the previous baseline templates so you can harden your system even more.

- Understand the dependencies of Exchange Server and general Windows operating-system services.

- Make the appropriate changes to service state as suggested in this chapter.

- Stay on top of security hotfixes and service releases for not only Exchange Server but Windows server versions as well.

- Subscribe to a security bulletin mailing list.

- Set Exchange to not resolve Internet email messages, so your users can easily detect a spoofed message.

- Enable reverse DNS lookups on Internet mail received so that you can verify the transmitting SMTP server's identity and the trustworthiness of a particular message.

- Set a maximum number of recipients per message.

- Set a maximum message size.

- Set a maximum number of messages per SMTP session.

- Set a maximum size of an SMTP session.

- Set storage limits on mailboxes and public folders so you can prevent an attacker from filling up disk space.

- Restrict SMTP access by IP address or domain.

- Ensure that your SMTP server is a closed relay so you can prevent spammers from taking advantage of your connection.

- Delegate Exchange permissions appropriately.

- Modify Exchange System Manager so that the Security tab is present in the Properties view of all objects.

Chapter 10

The key auditing strategies for this chapter for Windows 2000, XP, and Server 2003 users are:

- Logon and logoff events, which can indicate repeated logon failures and point to a particular user account that's being used for an attack.

- Account management, which indicates users who have tried to use or used their granted-user and computer-administration power.

- Startup and shutdown, which shows both the user who has tried to shut down a system and what services may not have started up properly upon the reboot.

- Policy changes, which can indicate users tampering with security settings.

- Privilege use, which can show attempts to change permissions to certain objects.

For Windows NT users, the chief auditing points include:

- Audit failures for logon and logoff events.

- Audit all file and object access events for files and directories of special interest or particular concern.

- Audit failures of use of user rights.

- Audit both successes and failures of user and group management privileges.

- Audit both successes and failures of security policy changes—especially successes, because they would occur rarely in legitimate practice.

- Audit failures in restart, shutdown, and system events.

- Audit failures of process-tracking events.

For all versions of Windows, the following items apply:

- Make searching easier by filtering events inside Event Viewer.

- Search on events that interest you at `http://www.eventid.net` to learn more about them.

- Understand why some events might not be recorded in certain error logs.

Index

A

access control list (ACL) entries
    setting for Exchange 2000 Server
        partitions, 138
Access tab
    in Default SMTP Virtual Server
        Properties dialog box, 146–147
account lockout policies
    setting for user accounts, 41
Account Lockout Policy
    viewing, 82
Active Directory Users & Computers
snap-in
    for setting up a logon time
        restriction, 43
    for security configuration, 80
    viewing the default domain security
        policy with, 82
Add Attribute dialog box
    configuring the quarantine policy in,
        119
Add Directory dialog box
    Include in Index? check box in, 130
Add IP Filter dialog box
    adding a quarantined web resource
        in, 120
address spoofing
    protecting against, 142–144
administrative and default pages
    items to delete for greater system
        security, 133–134
administrative groups
    assigning permissions to in Exchange
        2000 Server, 148–149
Administrator account
    configuring in Windows, 67
    importance of using care in
        renaming, 20
Advanced Security Settings dialog box
    showing the SACL for an object in,
        152
Advanced Settings dialog box
    enabling security logging in, 50

Alerter service
    recommended setting in Windows
        XP, 52
Allow System to Shut Down Without
Having to Log On selection
    disabling, 42
Altiris tools
    for network management and
        deployment, 34
anonymous logins
    disabling to harden functionality of
        NT, 21
ANONYMOUS USER account
    granting and revoking access to, 42
antivirus software
    buying correct for your Windows
        version, 25
Apache
    using instead of IIS to harden system,
        134–135
Application Layer Gateway Service
    recommended setting in Windows
        XP, 52
Application Management service
    recommended setting in Windows
        XP, 52
Attribute Information dialog box
    configuring the quarantine policy in,
        119
AU client. *See* Automatic Updates (AU)
client
audit account logon events option
    for auditing policies, 151
audit account management option
    for auditing policies, 151
audit directory service access option
    for auditing policies, 151
audit logon events option
    for auditing policies, 151
audit object access option
    for auditing policies, 152
audit policy change option
    for auditing policies, 152
audit privilege use option
    for auditing policies, 152